STREETER

OF

BOND STREET

Edwin Streeter. 1834-1923.

STREETER

OF

BOND STREET

PATRICK STREETER

The Matching Press
Harlow

Published by
The Matching Press
1 Waterman's End
Matching, Harlow
CM17 ORQ
Tel. 0279 731308

Printed in Great Britain by
Quadrant Offset
Riverside House
Dicker Mill
Hertford

British Library Cataloguing in Publication Data
Streeter, Patrick
Streeter of Bond Street: Biography of a Victorian Jeweller
I. Title
739.2709421

ISBN 0-9518664-1-9

CONTENTS

ILLUSTRATIONS

The front cover shows New Bond Street at the turn of the century.

LIST OF SUBSCRIBERS

Clare d'Adhémar
Le Comte d'Adhémar de Panat
David d'Adhémar de Labaume
John d'Adhémar
Charles K. Aked
Mrs. Edward Akerhielm
Firkan Ali
Le Comte d'Azémar de Fabrégues

Roger Baden Powell
Peter Beale
S.E.F. Beechey, O.B.E.
Reginald Beer
Michael Bethell
Lister Bolton
Guy Boney, Q.C.
Olivia Bostock
Julia Breed
The British Museum
Penelope Brittain
John Brocks
The Broome Historical Society
Maureen Brown
Mrs. Shirley Bury
Axel and Angela Busch

Tiffany Callis
Richard Chester-Master
The Clockmakers' Company
Michael Connell
Diana Coote

Paul and Tessa Dixon
Rupert Douglas Bate

Carl Ebers, F.B.H.I.
Dr. Dorothy Ericson

Mrs. T. Farran
Peter Fletcher

Peter Garner
Nicky Gilmour
Julian Godby
Col. Philip Gold
Richard de C. Grubb
Howard Guard

Brian Hanson
John Haynes & Co. Ltd.
Brian Hedges
Carol and David Herrera
Simon Hodgson
Jane Hudson

Images of Bishop's Stortford
Georgina Innes
Javed Iqbal
Nigel Israel
Ian and Sue Ivison

Annick Jauré

Alice and Jack Kellar
William Kelly

Julia Langton
Tim Le Blanc-Smith

Lord McAlpine of West Green
Terrence McGrenera
Sarah Machin
Alix Mason
Jeremy Mason
Peter Mather

Jonathan Mathews
John Miller

Maj. Patrick Ness
Lavinia Newman
Boris Norman
David Norman

Evangelia Papageorgiou
Mrs. Graham Peddie
Stephen Pollock-Hill
Anne Purchas

Patricia Ramsay
Louise Reed
Judy Rudoe

Anthony Sainthill
Diana Scarisbrick
Rita Shenton
Ronald Schindler
Susan Shrager
Marilyn Smith
Lorne Somerville

Andrew Streeter
Revd. David Streeter
Edward C. Streeter
The late George Streeter
Robert Streeter
Thornton Streeter

Blane Thompson
Richard Timmis
Bernhard Trotman
Moira Trotman
Carolyn Turk
Jeremy Turk

Wartski
James Webb
Revd. John Weir
Julian Were
Virginia Were
Michael Whitelock
Wynyard Wilkinson
Wimpole Antiques
George Wright

FOREWORD

It was in the early 1960s when I began to research into various aspects of the diamond, in particular the stories of famous historical gems, that I was fortunate to come across in a London bookshop, a copy of E. W. Streeter's *Great Diamonds of the World* - even more fortunate because it was a signed copy. I was fascinated by the tone of this delightful book, first published in 1882, and the wealth of information which it contained. Not long after, I bought another of Streeter's books, *Precious Stones and Gems*, this book, together with my earlier find, made me keen to know more of the author.

Many years later I was able to do this when I met Patrick Streeter, the great grandson of Edwin Streeter. It was not long before I suggested to him that he might consider the idea of writing a book about his ancestor, who clearly was a most interesting person. I am more than happy that he has done so because we now know more about Edwin Streeter.

At a time when the British Empire had probably reached the zenith of its power and influence in the world and when London was a city full of the literati and the glitterati of the day, Edwin Streeter played his own part, aptly recognised by the writer, Rider Haggard, in a reference to him in his popular romance *King Solomon's Mines*, published in 1886. Streeter's interests were worldwide, pearls from Australasia, rubies from Burma, sapphires from the United States, emeralds from Egypt and diamonds from South Africa. Furthermore, he engaged in a campaign to remedy what he considered were defects in the British hallmarking system for gold, his expertise and persistence in this matter ultimately leading to legislation. There was too a link between Streeter and the notorious *fin de siécle* period through which he lived; his own Counsel, Sir Edward Clarke, also represented Oscar Wilde at the first of his trials.

Patrick Streeter has written that Edwin Streeter lived a long, colourful, and eventful life. It is very satisfying to record that his descendant has faithfully portrayed this life.

Walberswick, January 1993   Ian Balfour

ACKNOWLEDGEMENTS

I would like to thank all those whose help made this volume possible. In particular, John Culme, whose *Directory of Gold & Silversmiths* provided a backbone to the undertaking. Also, Judy Rudoe, of the Department of Mediaeval and Later Antiquities of the British Museum, who inspired me to put pen to paper. Thanks must also go to the Worshipful Company of Goldsmiths and the Worshipful Company of Clockmakers, who both helped with the publishing costs.

I would also like to mention Caroline Crisford, Sir George White, Nigel Israel, Dorothy Ericson, Gail Hebblethwaite, Penny Brittain; David Beasley of the Goldsmiths' Company; Paul Hollis of Hancocks & Co. (Jewellers) Ltd., who allowed me to photocopy his firm's press cuttings, and Stewart Rayment, who searched the Patent Office Records.

Special mention should be made of Jenny Sowter, who typed the manuscript; Wendy Livingstone, who masterminded the production and Stephanie Hall, who did the editing, helped by Anthea Streeter, Lister Bolton, Michael Brown and Philip Arnold.

Finally, I would like to thank all those who risked their capital in subscribing to subscription copies.

Matching Green, March 1993   Patrick Streeter

CHAPTER ONE

37 CONDUIT STREET

To come to business, Good and I took the diamonds to Streeter's to be valued,
as we arranged, and really I am afraid to tell you what they put them at,
it seems so enormous.
H. Rider Haggard. *King Solomon's Mines.* 1885.

Edwin William Streeter was a man of contrasts. Born of humble origins, he gained considerable fame and fortune only to recede at the end of his long life to genteel poverty and obscurity. He initiated highly successful expeditions to Burma to exploit the ruby mines, and to Australia to open up the pearling beds, but also backed disastrous ventures, which became the laughing stock of the financial press, to seek emeralds in Egypt and sapphires in North America. Likened to a Victorian Harry Winston[1], he presided for thirty-seven years over a prosperous Mayfair jewellery emporium. He wrote a number of well received and authoritative books which today are often quoted, yet he put forward stories about the history of his family and his firm which are pure fiction.

Edwin Streeter was born in 1834 at Wrotham, Kent. His father was proprietor of the Spring Tavern in the village and before taking up that trade had been a carpenter. His grandfather had also been an innkeeper at the Chequers in nearby Igtham. His parents had three other children, two of whom did not survive infancy. His mother died of consumption when he was seven and his little sister, Sarah, then aged two, was farmed out to live with friends. She, sadly, was to dic of scarlatina five years later. In 1846 his father moved to Dover to take up the Providence Inn. In a letter written to the Goldsmiths' Company when he was 85, Streeter stated that he 'started in trade in 1847'. This fact is backed up by a short biography published in *Leading Men of London* in 1895[2] which stated, 'He came to London while still in his thirteenth year. Having completed his education, he entered upon the career which he had chosen.'

He may have stayed with an uncle, also called Edwin, who was working as a linen draper in Bond Street. One question has to be answered here. Did a man who wrote a number of well received books, in a charming literary style, full of

---

1 J.B. Hawkins. *Thomas Cole and Victorian Clockmaking*. Privately printed, Sydney, 1975.

2 *Leading Men of London: A Collection of Biographical Sketches.* British Biographical Company, 1895.

scientific and classical references, really leave school at twelve years of age? It would appear that this was quite a common phenomenon for the time and that such people educated themselves by reading profusely.

Fig. 1. Messrs. Howell and James' Establishment in Regent Street
where Edwin was employed in 1853

In 1853, aged seventeen, he joined Howell and James, silk merchants and retail jewellers of 5/9 Regent Street as a buyer and five years later he became manager for Harry Emanuel at 5 Hanover Square. The firm of Emanuel has a long and colourful history. For details see John Culme, *Directory of Gold and Silversmiths*, but briefly the story is as follows.

Joel Emanuel was born in Steinhart, Bavaria in 1765, the son of Emanuel Mendel. He established his business at 14 Bevis Marks in 1801 and later handed it over to his sons, Morris and Edward. Michael, another brother, was to take over from Morris and they were joined by a fourth brother, Henry. Edward must have stepped down and in 1843, a branch at 5 Hanover Square was opened and subsequently Bevis Marks closed. In 1846 Michael and Henry were involved in sensational bankruptcy hearings. One estimate put the debts as high as £228,000. Commissioner Holroyd of the Bankruptcy Court pronounced Michael innocent of any offence but described Henry as 'one of the most fraudulent men that ever appeared before the Court.' In summing up, the Commissioner said that the bankrupts:

> carried on a very extensive business as goldsmiths and jewellers; their house was one of the first in the trade in this great metropolis. The father and the brother of the bankrupts, who were previously in the business, had both retired with ample fortunes, and before the disclosure of the circumstances which led to this bankruptcy there was every reason to believe, from the extensive connections of the firm, their annual returns and large profits, that the bankrupts also would in a few years have realised an independence. The misconduct of one of the bankrupts caused a sad reverse. He did not confine his attention to his own lucrative business, but unfortunately embarked too deeply in the trade of speculation ...

Some of the money had been lost on the railways and in the exportation of preserved provisions.

Michael Emanuel, the innocent party, continued the business until he handed it over to his son Harry, who prospered up to his retirement in 1873, in which year he sold his lease to Streeter. Harry then embarked at the age of about 53 on an extraordinary second career of aristocrat and diplomat. He bought the title of Baron de Almeida from the King of Portugal and in 1880 became Minister Plenipotentiary of the Dominican Republic. The *Jeweller's Circular* of New York in 1904 reported:

> In the course of a recent letter for a Washington newspaper, the Marquise de Fontenoy tells the following interesting story of a well-known jeweller: The death of Baroness de Almeida at Paris recalls to mind a romance of the Diplomatic Service which commenced in a Bond Street jeweller's shop and closed in the Parisian Legation of a republic of the New World. The late Baron de Almeida, who predeceased his wife by three or four years, commenced his career under the name of Harry Emanuel, the son of a wealthy Bond Street jeweller in London. In 1858 he became the partner of E. W. Streeter, the world famed expert in precious stones, but a quarter of a century later sold out to his partner, whose business is now known as

'Streeters', and, transferring his abode to Paris, became, thanks to the judicious manipulation of coin, Baron de Almeida in the Kingdom of Portugal. Finding in 1880 that the negro republic of Santo Domingo was without a diplomatic representative in Paris, he offered to take upon himself the duties of minister plenipotentiary and to maintain a full-fledged legation, with secretaries and attachés, at his own cost, and without expense to the poverty-stricken republic. The latter jumped at the chance, and from that time on Harry Emanuel, Baron de Almeida, figured as Envoy Extraordinary of a negro republic which he had never seen or visited, officially at any rate, and likewise, in a measure socially, found himself on a footing of equality with the other Chiefs of Mission of the Foreign Diplomatic Corps in the French capital, being admitted by virtue of his office to a number of smart clubs, to which he would never otherwise have been elected. He died as envoy, and was accorded all the military honours due to the representative of a foreign state who has expired at his post, loaded with decorations, among them the Legion of Honour, the Portuguese Order of Christ, and the Order of St. Isabella, the Catholic, of Spain. His body was taken to England, and there buried in the Jewish Cemetery at Balls Pond, where his widow has now been laid in a grave beside him, for in spite of his diplomatic honours and his Christian orders of knighthood, he had never forgotten the ritual faith of his forefathers.

Harry was to die in Nice in 1898. In the same year Edwin married Sarah Grainger Skelton, the daughter of a surgical instrument maker. They were to have nine children, who all grew to adulthood. His address at the time was 6 Toriano Avenue, Camden.

In 1860 Emanuel purchased the stables of the Marquis of Downshire's former house in Hanover Square. This remarkable structure still stands, although the two upper floors are new, and is currently occupied by the National Westminster Bank. It is well worth a visit to see the gems forming the architectural embellishments on the façade. The *Illustrated London News* on 17 November 1860 described the building thus:

Mr. Emanuel's House, Brook Street, Hanover Square

The illustration on the first page represents one of the most unique and commodious buildings for business and domestic purposes at the west end of London. About five years since the present Marquis of Downshire sold the family mansion in Hanover Square to the managers and directors of the London and County Bank, which, having been modernised by various alterations and improvements, stands prominently forward as the most

Fig. 2. Improved street architecture: Mr. Harry Emanuel's new house of business in Brook Street, Hanover Square

imposing edifice in the Square. The stables which adjoined, and which were remarkable for their superior accommodation and extent, have been pulled down, and the site purchased by Mr. Harry Emanuel, on which he has built the spacious premises of the character of which our description will give some faint outline. Mr. C.O.Parnell, whose fame as an architect has been established by his designs (and their subsequent execution) of the Army and Navy Club in Pall Mall, the Great Hall in Liverpool, and other places, was the author of the plan. The frontage is about eighty feet in length, thus affording ample space to preserve uniformity in the extensiveness of the building. The material is red brick with stone facings, and, as will be seen by the proportionate characteristics of the engraving, most elaborately ornamented with stucco facings and large windows, sub-divided into two sashes only, each being glazed with single sheets of the best plate-glass. The base of the building in the interior is devoted to the strong iron and fireproof keeps, in which are deposited every night most costly jewels and precious stones, large chests of plate, etc; rooms for cleaning gold and silver plate; separate compartments for trade purposes, where business is conducted with other dealers in these valuable articles of commerce; dining rooms for the young men; kitchens and other domestic offices. On the ground floor is the shop, or showroom, which is approached from the hall by two massive folding doors. It is 50 feet in length, by 80 feet in width, and 19 feet in height. In the centre is a large stove, ornamental in its character, so as to resemble a gigantic flower-vase, and which, at this season of the year, is filled with full blooming plants. All the cabinets are made of ebony, and the many doorways are constructed of the same costly wood, with unusually large panels of plate glass. The ceiling is beautifully decorated after the most elaborate Elizabethan order, the cornices representing emeralds, rubies and amethysts in colours of green, crimson and purple. A single chandelier, with sun-burners, is suspended from the centre, and at night gives a brilliant appearance, as the cabinets are lined with chased and burnished silver articles of every conceivable variety. Ascending a flight of four steps, an entrance is given to the large plate-room, where a dinner service à la Russe is displayed in full and tempting elegance. On the same floor, and in immediate communication, are the diamond and model rooms, with various recesses, tables and desks, for the employees of the establishment. On the first floor is a whole suite of elegant rooms, suitable either for the purposes of a commodious dwelling-house or a more extensive display of the materials of the costly trade in which Mr. Harry Emanuel is engaged. At present it serves both purposes, as his representative, Mr. Streeter, is always resident on the premises, and, spacious as is the accommodation, the whole area seems quite absorbed by the uses to which it is devoted.

At the opening of the building Streeter moved in as resident manager and in the same year his first son, Harry Edwin was born. Sadly Emanuel was only able to stay at these premises for four years. Probably to reduce overheads he moved to 18 New Bond Street in 1864,[1] a premises to be taken over by Streeter some nine years later.

---

1 Culme, p.147.

Fig. 3. Half Crown Day at the London International Exhibition 1862. At the time E.W. Streeter, aged 28, was Harry Emanuel's Manager.

Fig. 4. One can speculate that the young employee holding a jewel-case in the centre of the stand might be him.

At about this date Francis Hancock and Richard Burbrook started in business as retail jewellers at 37 Conduit Street.[1] The business could not have been on a sound financial footing because two years later the partnership was dissolved and the estates of the partners wound up.[2] However, the firm was reconstructed as Hancock, Burbrook & Co. Ltd. In 1866 Streeter left Emanuel and joined them as manager.[3] Within one year he was able to take over the business and start trading as Edwin W. Streeter.[4]

It is not known how he found the finance to purchase this business but as it was in a parlous condition, he may well have bought it cheaply. We know that in 1859 he took a small shareholding in the Portland Co. Ltd.[5] formed by Harry Emanuel to exploit a new way of electro-plating goods and while he was living over the shop at Brook Street, his living expenses may have been small. He could have dealt in jewellery on the side and thus accumulated some capital. In an advertisement in *The Times* of 1 April 1868 the business is described as Hancock, Burbrook and Co. (Ltd.) now Edwin W. Streeter. However, in future advertisements and catalogues until 1873, the business is called Streeter, successor to Hancock and Co. Ltd. This may well have been to disassociate the name from that of Burbrook who was adjudicated bankrupt in 1872. In any case it was mischievous because confusion was caused by the firm being associated with that of C. F. Hancock then of Bruton Street, now of Burlington Gardens. In fact C. F. Hancock kept a file of press cuttings on Streeter and had to disassociate themselves from his activities on a number of occasions.

Starting early in his career, from about 1867 and for about twenty years, Streeter conducted a campaign on what he considered were the inadequacies of the British hallmarking system for gold. Gold is graded in carats, 24 carat being one hundred per cent pure, 18 carat being 18/24ths gold and so on down the scale.

---

1 Culme, p.208.

2 Ibid.

3 In 1867 he published his first book, *Hints to Purchasers of Jewellery* and on the frontispiece he is described as Manager of Hancock, Burbrook & Co. (Ltd).

4 Hancock and Burbrook were to try in business again. They traded from 14 Hanover Street but the partnership had to be dissolved and they were both bankrupted in 1872 (Culme, p.208).

5 Culme, p.370.

His main complaints were:

1. Metal could be used with gold content as low as nine carat and still be described as gold. Streeter advocated, and used, only 18 carat or more in his workshops.

2. The regulations allowed hallmarking of unfinished or hollow articles. This enabled them to be tampered with later. This practice was not allowed on the continent.

3. The Goldsmiths' Company never exercised its power of undertaking spot checks on retailers' stocks.

In 1866 he wrote to the Chancellor recommending reforms and in the following year published a little book, *Hints to Purchasers of Jewellery and Watches*. In this he stressed that, as hallmarks could not be relied upon, purchasers should always obtain an invoice from the retailer detailing the quality of the gold. In 1873 he held a well published conference at Conduit Street, where fraudulent pieces were exhibited.[1] The President of the Pawnbrokers' Association was present. Among the exhibits was a lady's elastic neck-chain, hallmarked 18 carat, the value, if genuine, being £11, which was made mainly of silver and red lead. A pawnbroker had lent £6/10/- upon it and its value was 22/-. An advertisement from an East End jeweller was produced offering to supply 'hallmarked gold rings to the public at 5/- each upwards' and a ring with his invoice was produced which, although bearing the 'hallmark', was full of cement.

In August of the same year the *Journal of the Society of Arts* announced:

HALL-MARKING OF JEWELLERY.— PRIZE FOR ESSAYS.

1. It having been brought to the knowledge of the Council of the Society of Arts that what is termed "Hall-marking" of jewellery and articles of gold and silver, is inadequate to secure to the public that protection in the quality of the materials for which it is intended, they have accepted the offer of one of the members, Mr. Edwin W. Streeter, to place £25 at their disposal, to be awarded as a prize for an Essay treating on this subject, with suggestions for an improved system.

2. The Essays must be sent in not later than the 1st of November, 1873, marked with a motto, or cypher only, accompanied by a sealed letter, with the corresponding motto or cypher marked outside, giving within the name and address of the writer of the Essay.

3. Brevity will be considered a merit.

4. The Council shall have the right of publishing the prize Essay in the *Journal*, and they reserve the right of withholding the prize altogether, or of awarding a lesser sum, if the judges shall so recommend.

P. LE NEVE FOSTER, *Secretary*.

---

1 *The Times*, 7 April 1873.

The competition was won by Alfred Lutschaunig, Manager of the Liverpool Assay Office[1] and author of a book on hallmarks published in 1872. Lutschaunig put forward his remedies as follows:

1. Complete abolition of the action and interference of the Goldsmiths' Company. The grievances against this company, shortly summed up are:- Nonfulfilment of duty; inability to devise a simple, practicable and rational method of control over the ever-increasing manufacture of jewellery; and a drowsiness of action as regards all innovations required by the altered state of things. I will add, that in the face of the present progress, the Goldsmiths' Company stands like an old dilapidated house in the midst of modern, handsome buildings.

2. The adoption of only three standards, 12 carats (articles to melt down to 11 carats), 18 carats (articles to melt down to 17 carats), 22 carats (articles to melt down to 21 carats).

3. Government inspectors to be appointed, with power to buy at fixed prices any articles in any stage of manufacture, at any time, from the jeweller's workshop, for the purpose of having them assayed. (The Factory Act then in force gave this power in other instances).

Next Edwin arranged for the translation from the German of *Gold: Legal Regulations for the Standard of Gold in Different Countries of the World* by Arthur von Studnitz and added an introduction and summing up. An article in the firm's catalogues was written by Professor Pepper[2] stating that if a piece of jewellery is made of 18 carat gold, it must necessarily be soldered with gold of less than 18 carats; it follows then that if the whole be melted together, the product must be something less than 18 carat, in fact generally 17 or $17\frac{1}{4}$. Streeter therefore used $18\frac{1}{2}$ carat gold and 16 carat solder so that the finished product never fell below 18 carats. The use of a touchneedle was advocated for testing the quality of the pieces.

---

1 This was not one of the statutory Assay Offices but probably an office attached to one of the Liverpool bullion dealers.

2 Professor John Henry Pepper (1821-1900) was lecturer and later director at the Royal Polytechnic in Regent Street. He was famous for 'Pepper's Ghost', a stage show utilising optical illusions. He travelled to Australia, Canada and America displaying his ghost and giving popular science exhibitions and lectures.

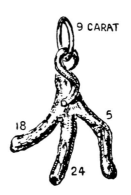

Fig. 5. The Touchneedle

Three Parliamentary Select Committees reported on the subject, in 1855, 1876 and 1879. The second two committees lamented the fact that no action had been taken on the recommendations of their predecessors but that the reformers had to wait until the Hallmarking Act 1973 for the modernization of the law. Edwin gave evidence to the 1879 Committee. He stated that the Goldsmiths' Company found hallmarking a trouble and currently they often damaged articles in the process of marking. He maintained that hallmarking should be the province of the Royal Mint. There should only be three compulsory stamps - a universal one for the metal, a date stamp, and a decimal one indicating the quantity of precious metal which should not be less than 18 carats. Also he pointed out the weakness in the law in that, unless there was a detailed receipt, only the Goldsmiths' Company could prosecute for fraudulent hallmarking and they were slow to do this. Any aggrieved individual should be able to prosecute.

The campaign was directed at both the Government, who made the statutes, and the Goldsmiths' Company, who carried them out. Edwin respected the Company, although he regarded them as old fashioned, as can be seen by these comments from the 1882 preface of his book, *Precious Stones and Gems*.

I trust that the Goldsmiths' Company as fathers of the trade, will ere long throw open their fine suite of rooms in Foster Lane. To them we must look for aids to the more general appreciation of fine art jewellery, by affording favourable opportunities for exhibitions and prizes, similar to those offered by the Turners' Company, together with gratuitous lectures, and the free use of their reading room to members of the trade. This would give an impetus to study to those engaged in jewellery-work, and enable the public to obtain a more accurate knowledge of, and a deeper interest in, a subject which has hitherto remained the property of an exclusive few. The legacies bequeathed to the Goldsmiths' Company by the famous jewellers of the 15th, 16th and 17th centuries, which have since increased in value to an extent almost inconceivable, without doubt were intended for some such purposes as those to which I have referred.

Once Streeter was established in his own business at 37 Conduit Street as a retail jeweller, he was set for years of continuous prosperity. He began issuing regular catalogues and up to the wind-up of the firm in 1905 at least 104 editions had been published. In 1869 he took over Aubert & Co., clockmakers of 252 Regent Street[1] and in the next year he was to organise his first prospecting expedition.

1 *The Times*, advertisement, 3 January 1870.

CHAPTER TWO

CATALOGUES, FREE FOR TWO STAMPS

The catalogues were sent free to applicants on receipt of two stamps. Indeed, the requirement of two stamps was dropped after a while. Antiquarian book dealers now ask over £150 for these catalogues.

The earliest edition seen by this author was issued in 1869. There are four sections: three on machine made jewellery, watches and clocks respectively and one on English bronze work. Great emphasis is made on the introduction of machines which, it is claimed, reduces the price but maintains the quality. Examples of the pieces put forward include an Etruscan ram's head, swinging pendant earrings for five guineas and Greek earrings with swinging beads for the same price. (Figs. 6 and 7).

Fig. 6.   Fig. 7.

Greek, Etruscan and archaeological styles were especially prevalent. Amongst the watches was a gold keyless horizontal one with gold dial and engraved case. The open faced version cost ten guineas and the 'hunter' or 'half hunter', fourteen guineas. (Fig. 8).

Fig. 8.

The clock section was comprehensive, covering Carriage, Ormolu, Boudoir, Library and Marble Volute clocks as well as Turret, Church and Stables ones. An eight-day lever Carriage Clock five inches high cost £5 (Fig. 9) and an Ormolu and Porcelain Boudoir clock fourteen inches high could be bought for £12 (Fig. 10).

Fig. 9.   Fig. 10.

Finally in this catalogue, under the heading 'English Bronze Work', it was announced:

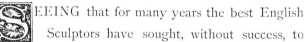

SEEING that for many years the best English Sculptors have sought, without success, to re-produce their works in Bronze, *(hence the entire absence of any Bronze Groups illustrative of English Sports and Subjects)*, Mr. STREETER has undertaken to edit a series of the best

ILLUSTRATIONS OF ENGLISH SUBJECTS,

By British Artists,

in the belief that the time has arrived when, in point of price and artistic finish, these Bronzes will successfully compete with the Bronze work of the Continent.

A spacious SHOW ROOM, devoted to the exhibition of such works, has been opened at the premises, 37, Conduit - street, Bond - street, and an inspection is respectfully invited.

Catalogue No. 14, which was issued a year or so later, advertised the manufactory, trade and wholesale entrance at the rear of the premises at 37 Coach and Horses Yard. A new inclusion was the Explorer's Watch which was keyless, watertight and sandproof. Also new were bridesmaids' suites and lockets. Individual items started at £5 and the set cost £50 (Fig. 11).

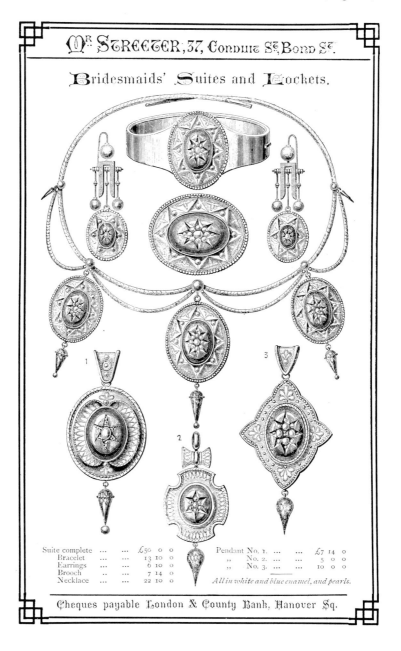

Fig. 11.

15

The 21st catalogue, issued around 1871, included features on diamond bracelets and head ornaments. The piece in Fig. 12 cost £250, or you could have your own diamonds mounted from, according to number, £40. The bracelet in Fig. 13 cost: centre and bands, £300; with gold bands and diamond centre, £100; centre alone, £85; and your own diamonds mounted, £50.

Fig. 12. Diamond Bird Head Ornament

Fig. 13. Diamond Bracelet

Links, pins and studs (Fig. 14) could be sent on approval.

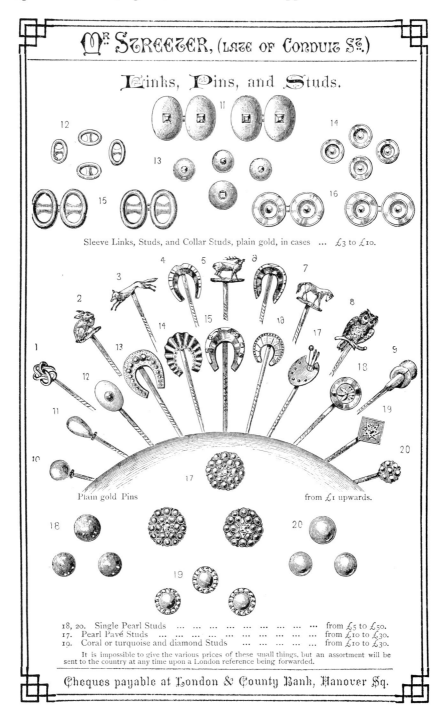

Fig. 14.

The 29th edition was issued at the time of the move to 18 New Bond Street. The manufactory had moved to Burlington Steam Works, Savile Row. A preface on diamonds announced:

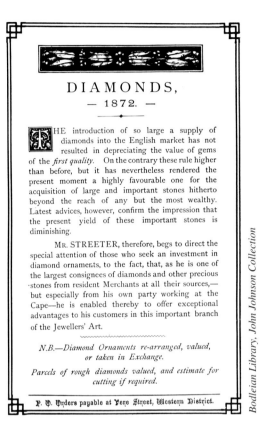

Diamond Jewellery was now added to machine-made gold jewellery. The earring in Fig. 15 cost £80; the locket in Fig. 16, £120.

Fig. 15.

Fig. 16.

The locket in Fig. 17 could be made in diamonds, rubies and diamonds or emeralds and diamonds from £35.

Fig. 17.

The range was innovative, as can be seen from the suite of *Owl in Ivy Bush* and the Patent Ring Pendant.

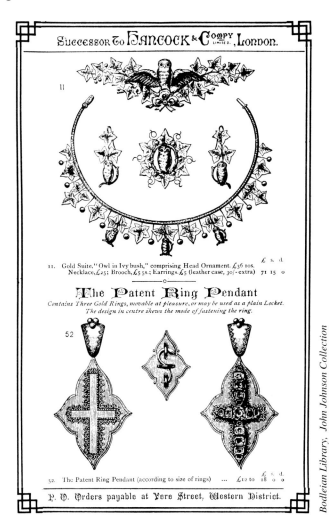

Fig. 18.

19

Mourning lockets were introduced (Fig. 19) but these did not feature in future catalogues so the demand must have been limited.

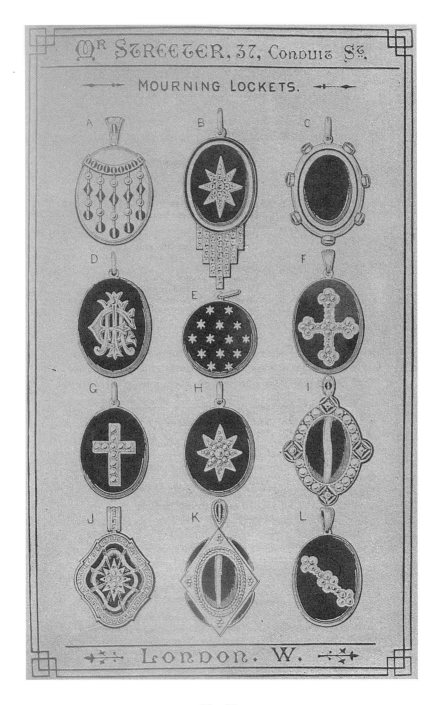

Fig. 19.

Thirty-four new pages were added to cover silver and plated goods, a selection of which follows (Figs. 20-31). Canteens were specially made for the Colonies of best seasoned oak.

Fig. 20.

Fig. 21.

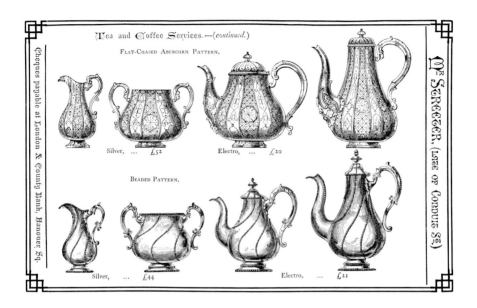

FLAT-CHASED ABERCORN PATTERN.

Silver, ... £52   Electro, ... £20

BEADED PATTERN.

Silver, ... £44   Electro, ... £21

Mr SCREETER, (LATE OF CONDUIT ST.)

Cheques payable at London & County Bank, Hanover Sq.

Fig. 22.

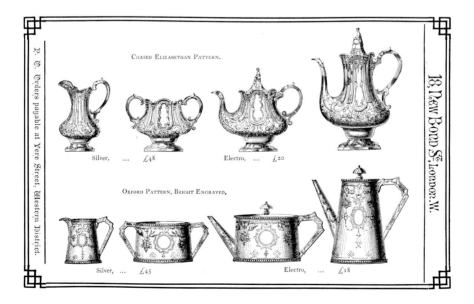

CHASED ELIZABETHAN PATTERN.

Silver, ... £48   Electro, ... £20

OXFORD PATTERN, BRIGHT ENGRAVED.

Silver, ... £45   Electro, ... £18

P. O. Orders payable at Vere Street, Western District.

18, NEW BOND ST. LONDON. W.

Fig. 23.

22

Fish-eating Knives & Forks.

Per Dozen.

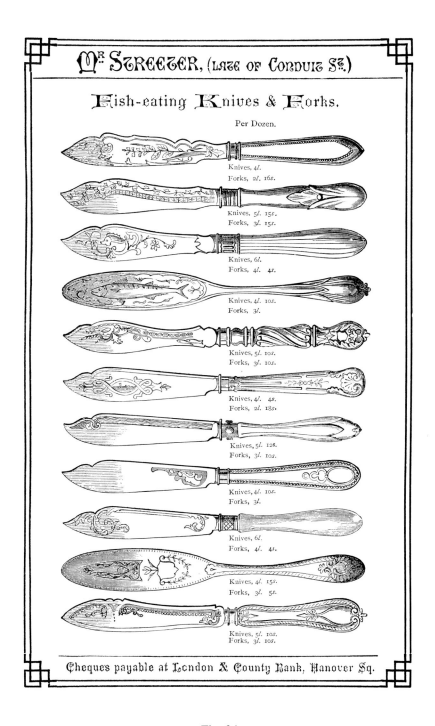

Knives, 4*l*.
Forks, 2*l*. 16*s*.

Knives, 5*l*. 15*s*.
Forks, 3*l*. 15*s*.

Knives, 6*l*.
Forks, 4*l*. 4*s*.

Knives, 4*l*. 10*s*.
Forks, 3*l*.

Knives, 5*l*. 10*s*.
Forks, 3*l*. 10*s*.

Knives, 4*l*. 4*s*.
Forks, 2*l*. 18*s*.

Knives, 5*l*. 12*s*.
Forks, 3*l*. 10*s*.

Knives, 4*l*. 10*s*.
Forks, 3*l*.

Knives, 6*l*.
Forks, 4*l*. 4*s*.

Knives, 4*l*. 15*s*.
Forks, 3*l*. 5*s*.

Knives, 5*l*. 10*s*.
Forks, 3*l*. 10*s*.

Cheques payable at London & County Bank, Hanover Sq.

Fig. 24.

23

Electro and Silver Fish Carvers.

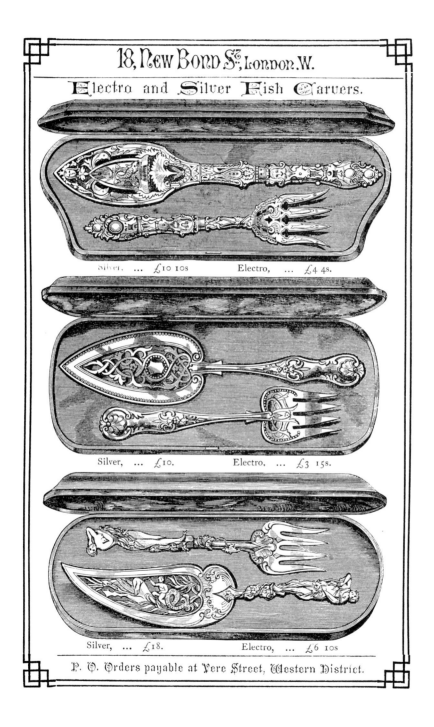

Silver, ... £10 10s   Electro, ... £4 4s.

Silver, ... £10.   Electro, ... £3 15s.

Silver, ... £18.   Electro, ... £6 10s

P. O. Orders payable at Vere Street, Western District.

Fig. 25.

Mr STREETER, (Late of Conduit St.)

Breakfast Cruets.

Silver, ... £7 10s.
Electro, ... £3 15s.

Silver, ... £18.
Electro, ... £6 15s.

Silver, ... £21.   Electro, ... £9 10s.

Silver, £5 10s.   Electro, £1 10s.

Silver, £6 6s.   Electro, £2 5s.

Cheques payable at London & County Bank, Hanover Sq.

Fig. 26.

Breakfast Cruets.—*(continued.)*

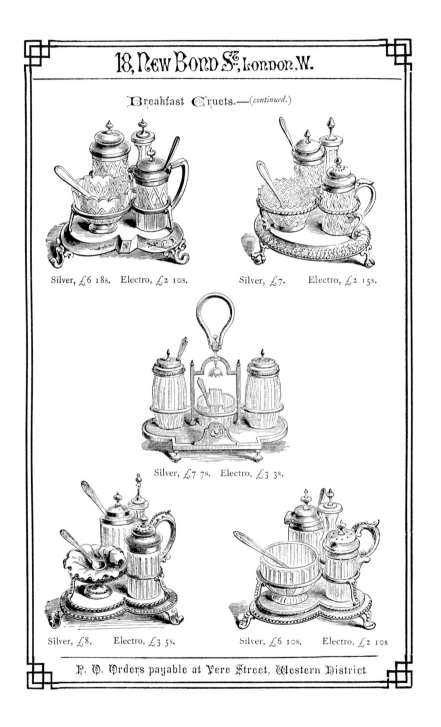

Silver, £6 18s.   Electro, £2 10s.   Silver, £7.   Electro, £2 15s.

Silver, £7 7s.   Electro, £3 3s.

Silver, £8.   Electro, £3 5s.   Silver, £6 10s.   Electro, £2 10s.

Fig. 27.

26

Beaded Pattern.　　Claret Jugs.　　Grecian Pattern.

Silver, £26.　Electro, £10.

FIGURE HANDLE.

Silver, £25.　Electro, £10 10s.

OTTER HUNT PATTERN.

Silver, £28.　Electro, £12.

Silver ... ... £36.

Cheques payable at London & County Bank, Hanover Sq.

Fig. 28.

Claret Jugs. — *(continued)*.

Silver ... ... £21.
Electro ... ... £9.

Silver ... .. £16 16s.
Electro ... £6 10s.

Silver ... £30.
Electro ... £14.

Silver ... £25.
Electro ... £10 10s.

Silver ... ... £45.
Electro ... ... £18.

P. O. Orders payable at Vere Street, Western District.

Fig. 29.

28

Candelabra.

Any figure can be supplied on base.

Fig. 30.

29

Fig. 31.

The 60th edition, issued some thirteen years later, differs surprisingly little from the one just described. Another steam factory in St. Brides Street E.C. was in operation. Chatelaines were introduced (Figs. 32 and 33) and the presentation plate section was well publicised (Figs. 34 and 35).

Fig. 32.

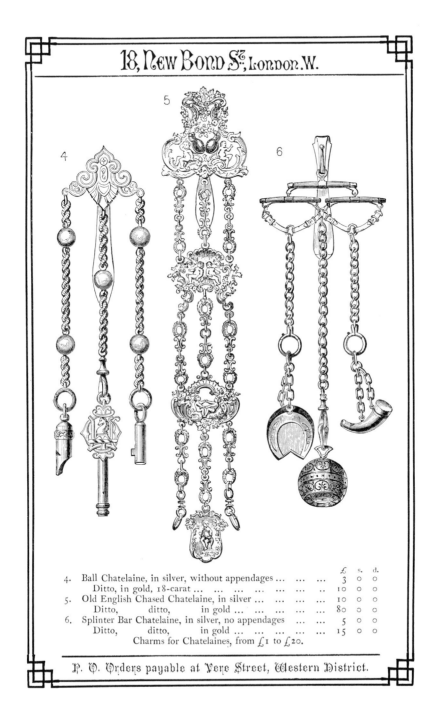

		£	s.	d.
4.	Ball Chatelaine, in silver, without appendages	3	0	0
	Ditto, in gold, 18-carat	10	0	0
5.	Old English Chased Chatelaine, in silver	10	0	0
	Ditto, ditto, in gold	80	0	0
6.	Splinter Bar Chatelaine, in silver, no appendages	5	0	0
	Ditto, ditto, in gold	15	0	0
	Charms for Chatelaines, from £1 to £20.			

P. O. Orders payable at Vere Street, Western District.

Fig. 33.

Chased Silver CUP, surmounted by Yacht, ...   £75.

For Prize Cup, any subject can be added, same price.

Fig. 34.

33

Silver chased TAZZA with Cover, £100.

Cheques payable at London & County Bank, Hanover Sq.

Fig. 35.

34

By 1898, when the 101st catalogue was issued, the format had radically changed. Colour printing was used, the gold being particularly attractive as it was printed using real gold. There were articles on all the different precious stones and one on the measurement of their hardness. The Victorian designs had been superseded by Edwardian. The firm's special knowledge on questions of heraldry was announced, one of the directors, Captain F. Manners, being an expert. Fig. 36 shows the diamond pendants.

DIAMOND PENDANTS.

1120.	All Diamond Pendant, also forming Brooch	...	...	...	...	£185	0	0
1121.	Opal and Diamond Heart Shape Pendant, also forming Brooch	...				100	0	0
1122.	All Diamond Pendant, also forming Brooch	...	...	...		120	0	0
1123.	Fine Diamond Collet Pendant, also forming Brooch	...	...			385	0	0
1124.	Pearl and Diamond Cluster Pendant, also forming Brooch	...				200	0	0
1125.	Diamond Collet Pendant, also forming Brooch	...	...	...		90	0	0
1126.	Opal and Diamond Pendant, also forming Brooch	...	...	...		100	0	0
1127.	Pearl and Diamond Five-Cluster Pendant, also forming Brooch	...				125	0	0
1128.	Opal and Diamond Oval Cluster Pendant, also forming Brooch	...				140	0	0

THESE DESIGNS ARE DRAWN TO ACTUAL SIZE, AND PRICES ARE QUOTED NET; SMALLER ORNAMENTS OF SAME DESIGN CAN BE HAD AT PROPORTIONATE PRICES.

Fig. 36.

There was a special section on amber (Fig. 37).

AMBER SPECIALITIES.

1302.	Gold mounted Amber Match Box, Gem push piece	£8 15 0
1303.	Gold mounted Amber Sovereign Purse	9 0 0
1304.	Gold mounted Amber Match Box, set with Rubies	25 0 0
1305.	Gold mounted Amber Match Box	10 0 0
1306.	Gold mounted Amber Bon-bon Box	6 15 0
1307.	Gold mounted Amber Stamp Box, set with Rubies	22 0 0
1308.	Gold mounted Amber Purse for Sovereigns and Half-Sovereigns ...	14 14 0

THESE DESIGNS ARE DRAWN TO ACTUAL SIZE, AND PRICES ARE QUOTED NET ; SMALLER ORNAMENTS OF
SAME DESIGN CAN BE HAD AT PROPORTIONATE PRICES.

Fig. 37.

The standard of printing in the 102nd edition of the catalogue was spectacular. The gold reproductions appeared as alluring as the real objects. Shown here is the page featuring ladies' fancy watches.

LADIES' FANCY WATCHES.

		£	s	d
1400. {	Sapphire and Diamond Watch	£35	0	0
{	Sapphire and Diamond Bar Brooch	28	0	0
1401.	Pendant Watch, Blue Enamel and Pearl, Diamond Centre...	11	15	0
1402.	Pendant Watch, Green Enamel Pearl and Diamond	14	15	0
1403. {	Ruby and Diamond Pavé Set Watch	80	0	0
{	Ruby and Diamond Fancy Bar Brooch	30	0	0
1404.	Pendant Watch, Fancy Enamel and Gold	7	5	0
1405.	Pendant Watch, Pearl Pavé Set	18	0	0
1406.	Pendant Watch, Pearl Border	7	15	0
1407.	Pendant Watch, Fancy Enamel and Pearl Border	7	15	0

THESE DESIGNS ARE DRAWN TO ACTUAL SIZE, AND PRICES ARE QUOTED NET; SMALLER ORNAMENTS OF SAME DESIGN CAN BE HAD, OR ANY GEM SUBSTITUTED FOR THOSE ABOVE AT PROPORTIONATE PRICES.

Fig. 38.

The gem flexible bracelets were set 'à jour' which meant that light could come through from the back of the setting, thus enhancing the design.

GEM FLEXIBLE BRACELETS.

ALL STONES SET " à JOUR."

1532

1533

1534

1535

1536

1537

1538

1539

1540

1532.	Pearl and Diamond Fancy Flexible on Gold Curb Bracelet	...	...	...	...	£60	0	0
1533.	Fancy Enamel and Diamond Flexible Bracelet	...	...	...	...	40	0	0
1534.	Sapphire and Diamond Flexible on Gold Curb Bracelet	...	...	...	...	45	0	0
1535.	Pearl and Diamond alternate on Gold Curb Bracelet	...	...	...	...	35	0	0
1536.	Fancy Enamel and Diamond Flexible Bracelet	...	...	...	...	35	0	0
1537.	All Diamond Flexible Bracelet	...	...	...	...	...	100	0	0
1538.	Ruby and Diamond Flexible Bracelet	...	...	...	...	75	0	0
1539.	All Diamond Flexible Collet Bracelet	...	...	...	...	195	0	0
1540.	Pearl and Diamond Collet on Gold Curb Bracelet	...	...	...	...	65	0	0

THESE DESIGNS ARE DRAWN TO ACTUAL SIZE, AND PRICES ARE QUOTED NET; SMALLER ORNAMENTS OF SAME DESIGN CAN BE HAD, OR ANY GEM SUBSTITUTED FOR THOSE ABOVE AT PROPORTIONATE PRICES.

Fig. 39.

There was a fine selection of gentlemen's and ladies' watches in this catalogue.

GENTLEMEN'S WATCHES

Gent's English Keyless Lever Watches, Brequet Sprung, Compensated for Temperatures and Positions, in 18-Carat Gold Extra Heavy Hunting and Half-Hunting Cases, or with Crystal Face, from £20.

In Silver Cases, from £8.

THESE DESIGNS ARE DRAWN TO ACTUAL SIZE, AND PRICES ARE QUOTED NET; SMALLER WATCHES OF SAME DESIGN CAN BE HAD.

Fig. 40.

LADIES' WATCHES.

Ladies' English Keyless Lever Watches, Brequet Sprung, Compensated for Temperatures and Positions, in 18-Carat Gold Extra Heavy Hunting and Half-Hunting Cases, or with Crystal Face, from £15.

In Silver Cases, from £6 15s.

THESE DESIGNS ARE DRAWN TO ACTUAL SIZE, AND PRICES ARE QUOTED NET; SMALLER WATCHES OF SAME DESIGN CAN BE HAD.

Fig. 41.

Fig. 42 shows the gold specialities.

GOLD SPECIALITIES.

1734.	Gold Match Box	£5 5 0
1735.	Gold Sovereign Purse	2 10 0
1736.	Gold Bonbonnière with Four Aces in Sapphires and Rubies, Diamond Centre ...	25 0 0
1737.	Green Enamel and Diamond Pencil...	6 0 0
1738.	Gold Cigarette Case...	12 0 0
1739.	Gold Twist Fluted Pencil	5 0 0
1740.	Red Enamel Pencil, Cabochon Ruby End	3 15 0
1741.	Gold Tube Case, with Gold-mounted Amber Cigarette Tube	3 3 0
1742.	Turquoise Enamel Pencil, with Turquoise End	2 15 0

THESE DESIGNS ARE DRAWN TO ACTUAL SIZE, AND PRICES ARE QUOTED NET; SMALLER ORNAMENTS OF SAME
DESIGN CAN BE HAD, OR ANY GEM SUBSTITUTED FOR THOSE ABOVE AT PROPORTIONATE PRICES.

Fig. 42.

41

The last catalogue that survives is the 104th edition published in 1900. This was dominated by the silver entries - jewellery taking up only 15 of the 136 pages. For the Victorian cleric there were three pages of pocket communion services. An example is given in Fig. 43.

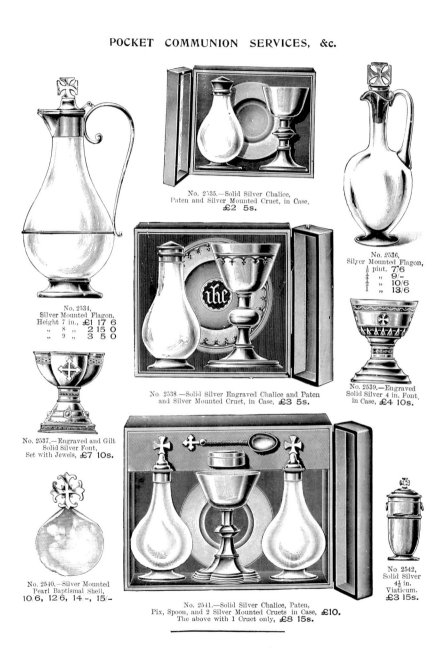

POCKET COMMUNION SERVICES, &c.

No. 2535.—Solid Silver Chalice, Paten and Silver Mounted Cruet, in Case, £2 5s.

No. 2536, Silver Mounted Flagon, ¼ pint, 7/6
⅓ „ 9/-
½ „ 10/6
1 „ 13/6

No. 2534, Silver Mounted Flagon, Height 7 in., £1 17 6
„ 8 „ 2 15 0
„ 9 „ 3 5 0

No. 2538.—Solid Silver Engraved Chalice and Paten and Silver Mounted Cruet, in Case, £3 5s.

No. 2539.—Engraved Solid Silver 4 in. Font, in Case, £4 10s.

No. 2537.—Engraved and Gilt Solid Silver Font, Set with Jewels, £7 10s.

No. 2540.—Silver Mounted Pearl Baptismal Shell, 10/6, 12/6, 14/-, 15/-

No. 2541.—Solid Silver Chalice, Paten, Pix, Spoon, and 2 Silver Mounted Cruets in Case, £10. The above with 1 Cruet only, £8 15s.

No. 2542, Solid Silver 4½ in. Viaticum. £3 15s.

Fig. 43.

From the silver displayed could be bought, looking rather like Tweedledum and Tweedledee, solid silver Muffineers (Fig. 44).

Fig. 44.

The catalogues, of course, only record the standard stock. For examples of one-off items that passed through the doors of New Bond Street and Conduit Street, we have to look at what is sold in today's auction rooms, to see what is in the nation's museums and private collections, and to search the stock of today's retailers.

In 1985 Christie's auctioned a gold mounted amethyst and chrysolite suite for £1,900 (Fig. 45).

Christie's

Fig. 45. Amethyst and Chrysolite Suite

Sotheby's sold a two-colour vinaigrette gold Rose Brooch. The bloom unscrews to reveal the receptacle (Fig. 46).

Fig. 46. Vinaigrette Gold Rose Brooch

Sotheby's

The same firm sold a gold, turquoise and half-pearl locket on a turquoise set bead edged necklace in 1986 (Fig. 47).

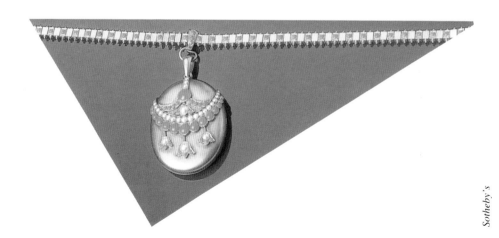

Sotheby's

Fig. 47. Gold Turquoise and Half Pearl Locket.

Hancocks & Co. displayed in their 1987 catalogue, a pair of cabochon garnet, gold mounted cufflinks with rope work borders (Fig. 48).

Fig. 48. Cabochon Garnet Cufflinks

Other craftmen's work that was sold by Streeter included a milk jug in the form of a fabulous monster in ancient Egyptian taste, having the body of a bird and woman's head, by James Barclay Hennell (Fig. 49).[1]

Fig. 49. Hennell Milk Jug.

---

1 Culme, *Nineteenth Century Silver.*

The Hull Grundy Collection[1] in the British Museum has some interesting examples of Streeter's work. Figs. 50 and 51 illustrate a brooch and pendant of gold, set with enamelled miniatures in Japanese style, each showing a figure in a garden, the gold settings bordered with emeralds, sapphires, rubies, opals and pearls.

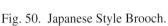

Fig. 50. Japanese Style Brooch.   Fig. 51. Japanese Style Pendant.

The sale of these items may have coincided with the exhibition of a Japanese Room displayed in his shop. The *Art Journal* in 1878 described it thus:

The public have been invited by Mr. Streeter to inspect the curious piece of architecture exhibited in a corner of his establishment as a Japanese apartment. It is a kind of bijou drawing-room, and constructed almost entirely of a sort of scented wood like cedar. The workmanship of the apartment is of the highest class, finished to the utmost degree capable, the wood being polished almost to the smoothness and brilliancy of glass. This polish is said to be obtained without the aid of either plane or burnisher. Whatever may be the method, it is certain that the result is marvellous. Every part is fitted exactly, without the use of a single nail, by means of sockets, grooves, and mortises. Three out of the four walls are formed so that one part may be slidden over another in the manner of some bookcases, and convert either wall at pleasure into a window or a doorway. The exceptional wall contains a peculiar recess fitted with a seat - the seat of the apartment. This seat has a special reserve and a peculiar significance. It is associated with the religious etiquette of Japanese life.

---

1 *The Art of the Jeweller.* Catalogue of the Hull Grundy Gift. Ed. Hugh Tait.

If a superior enter, even the Mikado himself, this would be his allotted niche. Hence it is considered sacred. But it could not be sacred unless it had that peculiar black unpolished pillar on the right, and that roof formed out of a single plank. These also are significant. Along the upper portion of the wall, and over the projecting sockets in which the sections slide, is a recess or groove, in which the owner is accustomed to keep his money. That, of course, is an extremely sacred spot. To an Englishman it is certainly a curious instance of the powerful effect of custom that so apparently insecure a depository should continue to be believed in or employed.

The Japanese, however, are a peculiar people. Domestic architecture among them is subject to the control of a sort of master of ceremonies, whose complex functions take the direction of prescribing not merely the code of manners, but the form and disposition of every room and closet in a mansion. His rule is absolute, being framed on a profound and mystical system of religious symbolism, in which everything means something philosophical or divine. This official seems to be a necessary adjunct to every palace or mansion, without whom nothing can be done. It is his duty to hire and pay all workmen, and to prescribe all duties of servants down to the minutest details. It is, moreover, a custom with the Japanese that every youth of quality shall serve an apprenticeship to this steward-architect-augur. Hence it is a competent office for any gentleman; and, as the Roman youth were all adapted by education to exercise the functions of lawyer and magistrate, so the youth of Japan are competent to fulfil the duties of this most important office of warden of the household and supreme source of etiquette. The identical chamber exhibited by Mr. Streeter was constructed for Dr. Dresser when residing in Japan, and has been passed over to the exhibitor because it is too large for the doctor's own house. Besides this apartment, Mr. Streeter has other Japanese curiosities - plates of inlaid silver of marvellous perfection, cloisonné enamels, jewellery, ancient vessels, all remarkable for some peculiarity utterly unfamiliar to the Western world.

Also in the Hull Grundy Collection is a bracelet of gold overlapping flexible links, set with turquoises in the form of a lizard (Fig. 52). The same Collection has a brooch in gold, die-stamped in relief with the Egyptian dung-beetle Khepri, the personification of Ra, the Sun-God (Fig. 53).

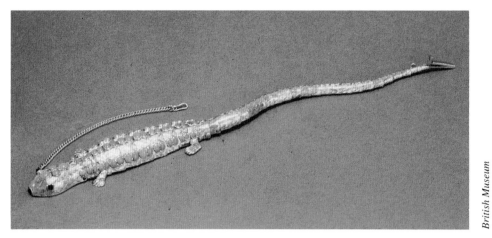

Fig. 52. Lizard Bracelet

Fig. 53. Dung-Beetle Brooch.

Fig. 54. Agate Locket.

The item in Fig. 54 is an oval gold and banded agate locket, centre set with a crystal reverse intaglio and decorated with eight banded agates. It was purchased from Silver of Burlington Gardens and is now in a private collection. Fig. 55 shows a double band bracelet with trefoil terminals joined by a meandering riband of diamonds. This item was recently to be found in the stock of Donohoe of Davies Mews, London.

Donohoe

Fig. 55. Diamond Band Bracelet

Nicholas Harris, formerly of Conduit Street, London, displayed the gold ram's head pin, marked *e.w.s.18,* (Fig. 57), at a recent exhibition. The set of six cravat pins, (Turquoise, Opal, Amethyst, Sapphire, Ruby and Pearl) (Fig. 56) are in a private collection, as are the gold locket and container (Fig. 58) and the gold enamel and pearl pendant (Fig. 59). Both these last two pieces are marked *e.w.s.18*.

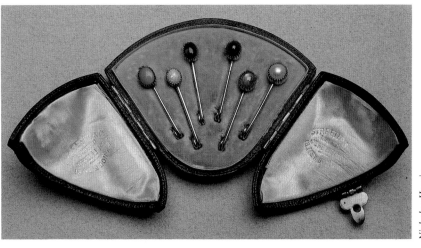

Nicholas Harris

Fig. 56. Set of Cravat Pins

Fig. 57. Ram's Head Pin.

Nicholas Harris

Fig. 58. Gold Locket

Bostock & Gerrish

Bostock & Gerrish

Fig. 59. Gold Enamel and Pearl Pendant

50

D. S. Lavender of Grafton Street recently had on display an eighteen carat gold King Edward VII and Queen Alexandra Commemoration Coronation Pendant, dated 26 June 1904, priced at £1,150 (Fig. 60).

Fig. 60. Coronation Pendant.

D.S. Lavender

On the other side of Grafton Street, Wartski were displaying a diamond pansy flower brooch, backed in gold, set in silver, with a price tag of £3,900 (Fig. 61).

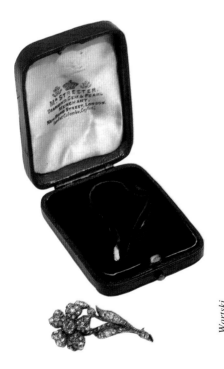

Fig. 61. Pansy Flower Brooch.

Wartski

Clocks sold by Streeter include an eight-day miniature carriage clock in a gilt case 3³/₄ inches high with box, for which Asprey were asking £3,850 in their Christmas 1988 promotions (Fig. 62).

Asprey & Co.

Fig. 62. Miniature Carriage Clock.

Derek Roberts Antiques of Tonbridge have recently had in stock a very fine porcelain-panelled gorge-cased carriage clock made by Drocourt of France. It has fine Sèvres panels decorated with semi-precious stones and pearls and, as retailer, is signed E.W.Streeter (Fig. 63).

Fig. 63. Drocourt Carriage Clock.

It would be worthwhile, at this stage, to look in more detail at the machine-made jewellery which Streeter claims that he introduced and which he publicised greatly. Full details of the machinery, mode of manufacture and objects produced were given in Part II of his *Hints to Purchasers of Jewellery, Eighth Edition* published in 1867 and they are reproduced here.

PART II.

How Jewellery is made by Machinery.

 now proceed to describe the manufacture of golden ornaments; and that this may be the more readily understood, I propose to trace the construction of one of the bracelets illustrated. (Plate I. fig. *b.*) Suppose a skilled workman be required to fashion

E

Plate I.   SUITES.—18-Carat Gold.

Machine-made, 10*l.* 10*s.*   Hand-made, 15*l.* to 25*l.*

How Jewellery is made.   35

❖➤✦❖

this pattern by hand, the process would be this: The necessary quantity of gold having been weighed out — the gold would probably be in a piece of about a quarter-of-an-inch in thickness — it would first be hammered to the required tenuity; then, having cut it into strips, the artificer would construct the flat portion of the bracelet which goes round the wrist, and make the chenille or raised edge; then he would model the centre ornament by means of the hammer and chisel, and cut out the

36   *How Jewellery*

❖➤✦❖

beads and fasten them on; lastly—he would solder the various parts together and add the joint and snap.

The construction would of course in this way occupy much time, and as it could only be accomplished by a skilful workman, the bracelet must necessarily cost a high price.

But now let us see what machinery can do to lessen both labour and price. In the first place, the gold, instead of

Fig. 64.

◆>>◄◆

being hammered into the required thickness, is passed through the steam *Rolling Machine* (Plate II. fig. *b.*) and can be pressed out to any extent in a few minutes. It is then, with the greatest rapidity, cut into strips by the *Cutting Press* (Plate II. fig. *f.*) A die (Plate IV.) having been prepared, (and everyone who has a monogram for his note paper knows how quickly and inexpensively dies are made) a strip of the gold is put into the *Monkey Press*,"— (Plate III. fig. A)—an apparatus of con-

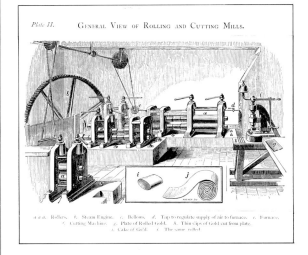

Plate II.   General View of Rolling and Cutting Mills.

a a a. Rollers.   *b.* Steam Engine.   *c.* Bellows.   *d.* Tap to regulate supply of air to furnace.   *e.* Furnace.
f. Cutting Machine.   *g.* Plate of Rolled Gold.   *h.* Thin slips of Gold cut from plate.
i. Cake of Gold.   *j.* The same rolled.

Plate III.

A

B

A. Monkey Press.   B. Lapping Machine.

◆>>◄◆

siderable power, and with two separate blows the two halves of the bracelet are stamped out. Meanwhile, by means of another die and *press of less power*, (Plate V. fig. D.) the centre ornament is with equal facility formed; and all that remains for the workman to do by hand is to joint the bracelet and put on the snap; and to polish it.

In the ornamentation of jewellery gold wire of different degrees of fineness is used. This wire is made as follows:

Fig. 65.

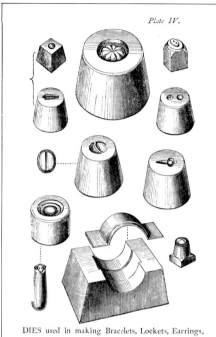

Plate IV.

DIES used in making Bracelets, Lockets, Earrings, Brooches, and Studs.

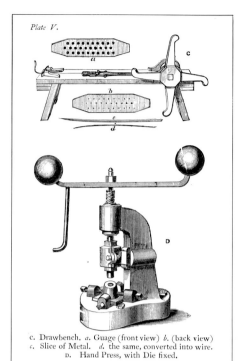

Plate V.

c. Drawbench. *a.* Guage (front view) *b.* (back view)
c. Slice of Metal. *d.* the same, converted into wire.
D. Hand Press, with Die fixed.

How Jewellery is made. 43

❖⊱✦⊰❖

The gold is first cut into strips by means of the *Cutting Press.* Each strip is then forcibly drawn through an aperture in a steel plate, which rounds it and forms it into wire. (Plate V. figs. *a. & b.* This is again passed through apertures, smaller and smaller, until the required size is obtained. These plates are called "*guages,*" and are capable of attenuating wire to any extent. It requires considerable power to force the strips through the guages, and this power is obtained by means of the *Drawbench,* (fig. c.) This

---

44   *How Jewellery*

❖⊱✦⊰❖

description refers of course to plain wire only; ornamental wires have to undergo an additional process.

A bracelet such as fig. *b.* would take a skilled workman *six* days to make by hand; whilst with the aid of the machinery I have described, the same ornament—including the necessary hand-work, such as jointing, polishing, &c.* — can be made in *two* days.

———

* The Lapping Machine (Plate III. fig. B.) is used for polishing the bright parts of gold ornaments.

Fig. 66.

❖➤◄❖

From the above brief description it will be readily understood how it is that really good jewellery may be obtained at a comparatively small cost, and yet a good profit may be had by the vendor. The price of the gold contained in any one ornament is the same, both to the jeweller and to the purchaser; the profit to the former is—or ought to be—derived from the workmanship, and the more quickly he can manufacture such articles, the cheaper he can sell them; getting for himself a fair profit, and

❖➤◄❖

giving to the public advantages which they could not have had under the old system.

In the following pages will be found the designs before alluded to.

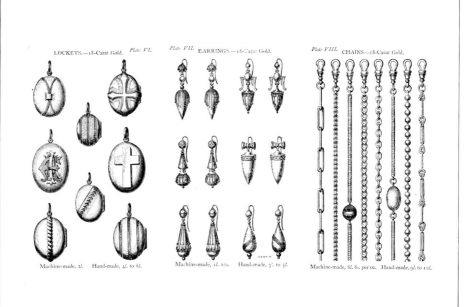

LOCKETS.—18-Carat Gold.   *Plate VI.*   *Plate VII.* EARRINGS.—18-Carat Gold.   *Plate VIII.* CHAINS—18-Carat Gold.

Machine-made, 2*l.*   Hand-made, 4*l.* to 6*l.*   Machine-made, 1*l.* 10*s.*   Hand-made, 3*l.* to 5*l.*   Machine-made, 6*l.* 6*s.* per oz.   Hand-made, 9*l.* to 10*l.*

Fig. 67.

CHAPTER THREE

18 NEW BOND STREET

Diamonds were first discovered in South Africa in 1866. There was no rush to exploit the find until three years later when the *Star of Africa* was found by a Griqua shepherd and sent to Europe to be exhibited.[1]

Streeter dispatched an expedition of three men under Thomas W. Tobin, Secretary of the Royal Polytechnic Institution. They left England on 23 November 1870 and arrived at the fields on 20 March 1871. Rhodes first arrived at the fields in September of that year and Barney Barnato three years later.

The *Diamond Field*, one of the local newspapers, announced on 27 April 1871 that Tobin was in Hebron and had been commissioned by the *Illustrated London News* to do sketches of the scenery. In May we find him lecturing 'About Diamonds' in the Diggers' Church Tent at Pniel and again in Cape Town in August.

In April, he sent a report back describing the geography, geology and the current method of working of the mines.[2] He stated that three good diamonds had already been found and that he considered that the best gems were to be found in the river bed. It was planned to send out machinery to enable the river bed to be exploited but at this point the whole expedition collapsed. Various reasons are given for this. Streeter himself says that it was due to the ill health of the leader Mr. Tobin.[3] The *Watchmaker, Jeweller and Silversmith* recounted in 1923 that Tobin, after finding a few diamonds, struck barren rock and sold the claim to an Australian for £500.[4] The same journal in 1904 connects the name of Russell with the project.[5]

---

1 In fact the delay was caused by Harry Emanuel who, in 1868, sent out Professor Robert Gregory, a member of London University, who published a discouraging report in the *Geographical Magazine*.

2 Letter Tobin to Streeter, 13 April 1871. Royal Geographical Society, printed in Appendix 1.

3 *Precious Stones and Gems*, E.W. Streeter, 6th edition, p.74.

4 *Watchmaker, Jeweller and Silversmith*, November 1923, p.1839.

5 Apparently the individual involved was the son of Henry Russell, composer of *A Life on the Ocean Wave* and *Woodman, Spare that Tree (W.J.S.* 2 April 1904, p.425).

The biography in *Leading Men of London*[1] merely states that had Tobin followed instructions, the wisdom of which had been fully demonstrated, the success of the expedition would have been assured. Frederick Boyle, an early eye-witness of the mines, ridiculed the expedition in his book *To the Cape for Diamonds* written in 1872. He wrote, 'Mr. Tobin is credibly reported to have reached the conclusion that ostriches carried our treasures to the spot'. An article, probably inspired by Streeter himself, in the London based periodical *South Africa* in 1895 states 'It was Mr. Streeter who satisfied the world that there were diamonds to be found in South Africa. He sent out a representative to purchase, who not only purchased, but bought claims and worked them; and so that matter was set at rest.'[2] Whatever the reason for the premature end of the expedition, a golden opportunity to be in on the early exploitation of the South African diamond fields was missed, a mistake that was not made, as we shall see, with the ruby mines of Burma and the Australian pearl fisheries.

On becoming a sole proprietor Streeter moved from living above the shop and set up household with his growing family at Foljambe House, Adelaide Road N.W. The Conduit Street business flourished and soon he was able to open a factory at the Burlington Steam Works, Savile Row.

In 1870 we hear of his first recorded trip abroad. He was asked by a London syndicate to travel East to value a large quantity of jewels which were to act as security for a War Loan. On the way out he stopped at a German town to purchase some jewels which had been recently valued for probate but which were not easily sold on the market. He took the jewels at valuation. They included an old Russian brooch at £4. In the centre appeared to be a piece of haematite which was in fact a fine round black pearl of 77 grains. The colour had faded in the sun. It was brought back to London, the outer layer was removed and a perfect black pearl of 67 grains appeared. It was sold on for £400 but Streeter heard that in Paris there was an exactly matching one. He bought it back for £600 and then sold it at a large profit to a Paris crown jeweller who sold the pair to a rich iron merchant for 50,000 francs (£2,000).[3]

---

1 *Leading Men of London: A Collection of Biographical Sketches.* British Biographical Company, 1895.

2 *South Africa.* 23 November 1895.

3 Streeter, *Pearls and Pearling Life,* p.269.

MR. THOS. WM. TOBIN,

Secretary and Lecturer, Royal Polytechnic Institution, London.

(BY PARTICULAR DESIRE,)

WILL DELIVER A

LECTURE,

On Saturday, the 6th May, 1871,

AT EIGHT O'CLOCK, P.M.,

IN THE DIGGERS' CHURCH TENT,

PNIEL,

ABOUT DIAMONDS,

THEIR ORIGIN & HISTORY,

Describing some of the many interesting incidents connected with the precious gem. The Country and Characteristics of the Diamond districts of South Africa—The Source of the Vaal—The Geological nature of the various Diamond localities—The Matrix or Birth-place, and best Diamond Fields—Some facts on the value and treatment of Diamonds generally.

THE LECTURE WILL BE

ILLUSTRATED BY DIAGRAMS.

Afterwards will be exhibited a series of

Dioramic Views!

OF THE

FRANCO-PRUSSIAN WAR!

Illustrative of the principal incidents of the late struggle, and the various Battles fought.

WITH EXPLANATORY REMARKS,

PROGAMME OF VIEWS:—

Saarbruck—and Baptismal Fire of the Prince Imperial.	Storming of Sedan
Weissemburg.	Interview between the King of Prussia, and Emperor of the French,
Battle of Woerth.	Strasburg.
Battle of Forbach.	Burning of Village of Bazeilles
Battle of Pange.	Paris in a state of Siege.
Battle of Vionville.	
Metz	

PORTRAITS:—

King of Prussia, and Emperor of the French.

Together with other interesting views connected with the Campaign.

Admission, 2s. 6d.

Doors open at Half-past Seven; to commence at 8 o'clock.

Tickets to be had at all the Principal Stores.

Fig. 68. Advertisement for Mr. Tobin's lecture, Pniel.

An interesting trip not as far afield but to Deptford was recounted by E.W. Streeter in the *Pall Mall Gazette*, 5 December 1885.

I remember years ago, just after the fall of Pekin, a suspicious fellow called upon me, and taking me aside, said he had just returned, and had something to show me. 'Where is it?' I said. 'Down at Gravesend'; and a day or two afterwards, having got to the rendezvous, a friend and myself set out down the river, each with his revolver. We got down, went to a house in a low quarter, and were passed into the man's bedroom, where he was living. 'Now, my man, what have you got?' He said, 'Come here and I will show you,' motioning me to go behind the bed. I didn't quite like it, but he reassured me; and when he had me face to face, keeping my eyes on him, and my hand on my pistol, he let down his trousers and bade me put my hand on a belt which was strapped round his waist. 'I want £20,000 for that,' he said, softly. 'Will you give it?' After some persuasion, he opened the belt, and poured out a shower of diamonds which lighted up the shabby room. 'Where did you get them from?' He refused to say, and after some bargaining we came to terms. He handed me the diamonds, and then I turned round and said, 'Now, my man, if you will call ——-, my bankers, you will find a cheque ready for you at 10 a.m. tomorrow morning. But before that I must have references and an account'. He gave them to me without a murmur, and I found them all right.

In 1873 Streeter applied for a patent for a 'carriage communicator' which was to make redundant the check-string and speaking tube in a brougham. There was a dial in front of the passenger and another in front of the driver. The dials indicated 'Go on', 'Stop', 'Right', 'Home', 'Club' etc. The passenger could then easily communicate his wishes to the driver. *The Times* quizzically suggested that as an improvement the dial be put in front of the horse and that the hapless animal be trained to read the indications.[1] It is believed that the invention did not catch on.

---

1 *The Times,* 24 October 1873. There is no record in the Patent Office of the application so it must have been unsuccessful. However Streeter was later granted the following patents:

1891	6,246	Separation of metals and precious stones from gangue
1893	6,804	Improvements in or connected with whistles or calls
1893	6,805	A new shade for lamps or candles, especially suitable for incandescent electric lamps

A more significant development of 1873 was the move to 18 New Bond Street.[1] Harry Emanuel, Streeter's old employer, had decided to retire and was to go to Paris to start a new career as a dubious aristocrat and diplomat.[2] Emanuel sold his stock at Christie's in December 1873 and at the same time Streeter moved into his premises which were a few yards from his old ones. The mechanics of the move can be seen from the plan which comes from the 1873 catalogue (Fig. 70).

With the move to 18 New Bond Street the growth and prosperity of the business continued apace. It might be useful to examine the reasons for this. Streeter had a flair for publicity. He advertised heavily and had the knack of getting his name regularly in the Press. The catalogues, two or three of which were produced every year, were widely distributed. Many of the press advertisements had an air of romance about them. In *The Times*, 27 February 1889, pearls are advertised direct from the pearling fleet and precious stones direct from the mines.

Fig. 69. New Bond Street at the turn of the century
No. 18 can just be seen on the right with a white awning

---

1 The building had earlier been Steven's Hotel, a haunt of Byron, Scrope Davies and Hobhouse.

2 See pp. 3-4.

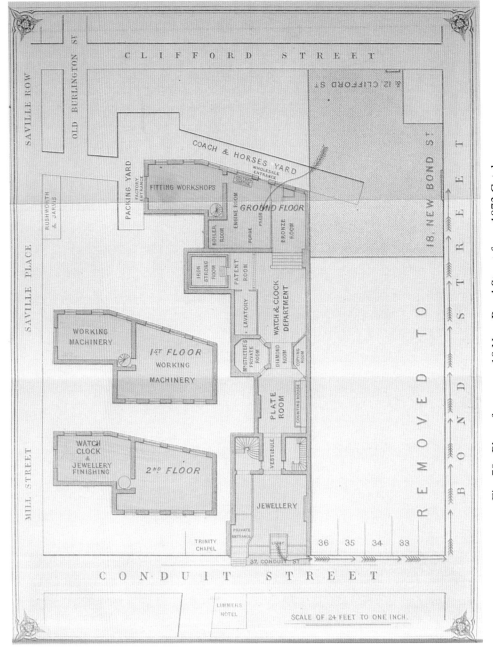

Fig. 70. Plan of move to 18 New Bond Street from 1873 Catalogue
(Note that plan is not strictly accurate as the old and new premises were not adjacent)

Fig. 71. Advertisement. *Illustrated London News.* October, 1886

We find him becoming involved in at least two exhibitions. The *Art Journal's catalogue of the 1872 International Exhibition* in London illustrates his contribution thus:

THE ART-JOURNAL CATALOGUE OF

Mr. EDWIN W. STREETER, goldsmith and jeweller, of Conduit Street, exhibits a large and very costly collection of jewels, remarkable for refinement and accuracy

of the pendants is so contrived that rings

may be detached from it; yet it will remain

an object of beauty. It is needless to add that all these jewels contain gems of great

of finish, and of very high merit as works of Art. In many instances they manifest much originality as well as grace and purity of design; and the case in which they are

rarity and value, "precious stones" worthy of rare setting. Our space is so limited that

shown supplies evidence of judgment and taste in arrangement. We engrave several examples, comprising PENDANTS, BROOCHES, a NECKLACE, and a TIARA. One

we may not attempt to describe them. They are valu- able acquisitions to the International Exhibition.

Fig. 72. The display in the 1872 International Exhibition Art Journal catalogue.

66

He also advertised in Charles Dickens' *Dictionary of London,* published in 1879, and placed advertisements on the front of the monthly instalments of Dickens' works when they were first issued.

Fig. 73. Charles Dickens' Monthly Editions.

Mysteriously, however, the *Journal* goes on to report that 'the contribution has, we regret to say, been withdrawn from the Exhibition through an unfortunate misunderstanding with the authorities, into the merits of which it would be out of place to enter here.' Better organisation prevailed at the Colonial and Indian Exhibition of 1886. The Australian arm of Streeter's enterprises (see Chapter 4), exhibited in the Western Australian Court, a diving dress, a cabinet of coral, a collection of pearls and various gems.

Fig. 74. The Western Australian Court at the Colonial and Indian Exhibition, 1886.

An example of Edwin's panache is the publicity he gave to his safe in Conduit Street. It is worth quoting direct from the 14th edition of his catalogue.

THE PATENT HYDRO-PNEUMATIC SAFE

The Hydro-Pneumatic Safe has been erected by Mr. Streeter for the safe custody of his own Stock of Jewels; but having been solicited by many customers, (who have long felt the want of a suitable depository when leaving town, for jewels, plate, deeds etc.), he is prepared to receive such property at a small fixed rate per annum.

This Safe is the largest hitherto erected, a Safe Room, in fact, fire-proof and thief-proof. Attached to it is an apparatus by means of which any interference with either of its walls - whether on each side, at top or bottom - is immediately detected. Thus an attack - even from the most experienced burglar, and under the most favourable circumstances - must end in failure.

The description of the Safe is here appended.

The Foundation
The original soil - gravel - having been first rammed down to make it as solid as possible; a bed of concrete 3-ft deep, formed of large pieces of hard clinker, bricks, granite, etc. mixed with cement, was laid over it; upon this was placed a bed of pure Portland cement, 3-in thick; then the Pneumatic tanks; another bed of cement, 3-in thick; and lastly, the Foundation plates of the Safe proper; making in all five distinct foundation layers above the soil.

The Sides and Back
Are surrounded by the following buildings: on the north, a Chapel; on the south, Mr. Streeter's Engine-room - the Boiler adjoining the wall next to the Safe; on the east, Mr. Sedley's Premises; the front of the Safe forming the west side, next to the shop. Leaving out the front and top, it is evident, therefore, that the only possible means of felonious entry are through the Chapel, Mr. Sedley's premises, or the foundation; which, to say nothing of party walls, would involve penetrating successively through 15-in of flint and Portland cement-concrete of the hardest description; the Hydro-Pneumatic Envelope; another bed of 12-in concrete; and, lastly, the Safe.

Fig. 75. The Safe at Conduit Street.

The Hydro-Pneumatic Envelope

Messrs. Chatwood, whose Safes remained invincible - notwithstanding their offer of £600, at the Paris International Exhibition of 1867, to any one who could penetrate them, - have guaranteed to Mr. Streeter, that by no portable appliance can an opening large enough to give admission be effected in either side of their safes in less than 48 hours; in front in not less than a week; and the concrete would take at least some 24 hours to work through. So that a burglar would have to be at work at the weakest point 72 hours, unobserved, before entrance was possible. Whereas the Hydro-Pneumatic envelope ensures immediate detection on being tampered with, either above or below ground.

This envelope consists of galvanised Tanks, perfectly air-tight, which are placed in the foundations and sides lying near neighbouring buildings; each Tank being capable of isolation at will, and in communication with the front, where an index gauge is attached to it. These tanks are filled with water, and being air-tight, the water-level is, of course, maintained without variation as long as they remain undisturbed, and instantly affected on the admission of air.

Simple as this may appear, it constitutes, as will be seen, an efficient means of detection, which is its sole object. It is not intended to serve as a material obstacle, the Tanks not being of extraordinary strength; but any interference with them would be immediately indicated by the gauge, while the operator had as yet 50 or 60 hours work between him and the interior of the Safe. If the pipes are cut, the air, under tension, escapes; if the tanks are broken, the water, also under pressure, escapes; and the index must, in either case, show the fact instantly.

The gauges require no setting after once being registered; under tension also, they indicate, by returning to a normal state, when anything is out of gear. Each of the Tanks has its own indicator, thus pointing out not only the existence of danger, but its locality.

The Front and Door

Access to the Safe is obtained by a doorway, 6-ft 3-in by 3-ft and 8in thick; the Door and Frame weigh 5 tons; it is constructed of, 1st. The outer thickness of best iron, the back of which is intersected with thousands of cones, to receive. 2nd. 'Spiegelised' Iron. 3rd. $\frac{1}{2}$-inch Plate iron. 4th. The lock and machinery, and the inner fire-proof covering.

The front of the Safe is 18-inches in thickness, and with the substitution of fire-brick for the 'Spiegelised' Iron, is constructed on much the same principle.

To obviate the necessity of wielding so massive a door each time the Safe is opened, there is an inner gate of iron, closed with a combination spring lock which gives ventilation during the day, and admits of inspecting the interior.

The lock is very large, capable of several thousand different combinations, which render the theft of the key useless. The size of the key is that in use for an ordinary cash box, and no other can possibly open the lock; it is also capable of division, and the different parts are kept by different persons.

The Top
Consists of 4-inches of iron, 16-inches of concrete, and 6-inches of Portland cement; making in all a thickness of 26-inches; and is in full view from the shop day and night, having a lamp lighted over it at night, which is regularly watched with the rest of the premises.

The Safe
The construction of the safe is different in principle from any previously attempted. It is in accordance with one of Mr. Chatwood's Patents for the 'building and binding together of cast Iron or Steel Plates'. So large a chamber could only be constructed in parts, and the problem of how to join these parts together so as to make a practically perfect whole, has been solved by Mr. Chatwood in the following manner: - A number of plates $3\frac{1}{2}$-in thick, of the best iron, weighing each several tons, and extending the whole transverse width and height of the safe are bedded or keyed into iron standards or ribs, about 4-inches square, known technically as 'H' iron, and these ribs are again keyed into each other at the angles; while, to make the whole mass compact, wrought-iron bars are screwed on in every direction from the inside, in a manner similar to that in which coupling irons are used in attaching locomotives and carriages together on the railways. By this treatment the pieces are made to form so nearly one mass that, adequate force being provided, the safe might be moved bodily without in any way deranging its construction. The weight of the Safe, without its surroundings, - taking the metal only - is between 50 and 60 tons.

The dimensions of the safe are as follows:

Height	9-ft. 6-in.
Width	9-ft. 0-in.
Depth	15-ft. 0-in.

This Safe, with its Hydro-Pneumatic Envelope, has been pronounced by the Public and the Press to be, in every sense - Invincible.

One would have thought that to publicise such an exact specification would be a gift to any Victorian safecracker! And as an added bonus, the exact location of the safe was shown in the plan of the premises in the 1872 catalogue. However there is no record of the fortress being penetrated.

Two years earlier there had been an unsuccessful attempt to defraud Streeter. He wrote thus to *The Times* on 13 December 1872 to warn his fellow tradesmen:

WARNING TO JEWELLERS
To the Editor of the Times

Sir, A well-planned attempt to swindle me out of a large quantity of diamonds and other precious stones has just been made by a firm in Rome. Their letter, containing the order, was written in such a manner that the most careful tradesman might have been deceived, and was followed up by another containing five foreign bills of acceptance, amounting to about 26,000 francs, as payment. These bills bearing well-known names, had, to all appearances been negotiated by different parties. Having a slight suspicion that all was not right, I determined on not parting with any of my goods until the bills had been presented. The following extract from a letter from my banker's agents at Bordeaux shows that my suspicions were well-founded. By inserting this in your valuable paper you will confer a favour and prevent further attempts being made by the same parties.

I am, Sir, your obedient servant,

EDWIN W. STREETER
37, Conduit Street, W.

MR. STREETER'S BOND STREET JEWEL STORE.

Fig. 76.

THE MUSEUM OF RARE GEMS AT STREETER'S.

Fig. 77.

73

Extract from Agents' letter at Bordeaux, Dec 9

We now beg to return you, enclosed, your two last remittances on Bordeaux, which are, we regret to say, forgeries. M. Ashue, whose name appears, states he knows none of the signatures. This startling incident made us look at the other bill which you hold from the same endorsement, 'G.G. Riccardi' and we have been informed this bill is also a forgery. You will probably never hear more from the party, who has, no doubt, tried to swindle you - unsuccessfully, we trust. On the whole it is a well got-up affair, and they have a good supply of seals, impressions, etc.

Returning to Streeter's flair for showmanship, Leopold Claremont, the lapidary, worked for him in the 1890s. Two large mahogany work benches were placed in the shop window and Claremont would cut jewels on these to the intense interest of passers-by.[1]

The Museum at Bond Street was another draw for customers. The 10th edition of the catalogue invited 'those who take an interest in gems to visit the Museum in the atelier at New Bond Street, where specimens of every known gem, both in the rough and cut, may be seen. From this collection, unique in its kind, purchasers may choose their own stones and have them set under their personal direction and to their own design. Collections of Precious Stones and Gems, in the rough or cut, arranged to order from £5 to £5,000.' We shall see in the Tasker case how the Museum was to prove a magnet for customers.

An article published in *Women at Home* in 1895, describes 'a long row of glass cases, containing specimens of every known gem in all its stages from the mine to mounter'. Also mentioned are 150 sapphires, each of a distinct colour. One case contained models of many of the great diamonds of the world. The facsimiles were cut in crystal and glass and tinted to match the originals.[2]

Similarly displayed were models of the *Gates of the Holy City* and of *Aaron's Breastplate,* both set with precious stones as described in The Bible. The relevant verses are:

Revelation 21: 18-21:

18. And the building of the wall of it was of jasper; and the city was pure gold like unto clear glass.

---

1 *The Gemmologist,* February 1932, p.214.

2 *Great Diamonds of the World,* p.291.

19. And the foundations of the wall of the city were garnished with all manner of precious stones. The first foundation was jasper; the second, sapphire; the third, a chalcedony; the fourth, an emerald;

20. The fifth, sardonyx; the sixth, sardius; the seventh, chrysolyte; the eighth, beryl; the ninth, a topaz; the tenth, a chrysoprasus; the eleventh, a jacinth; the twelfth, an amethyst.

21. And the twelve gates were twelve pearls: every several gate was of one pearl: and the street of the city was pure gold, as if it were transparent glass.

and Exodus 39: 8-19:

8. And he made the breastplate of cunning work, like the work of the ephod; of gold, blue and purple, and scarlet, and fine twined linen.

9. It was foursquare; they made the breastplate double: a span was the length thereof, and a span the breadth thereof, being doubled.

10. And they set in it four rows of stones: the first row was a sardius, a topaz and a carbuncle: this was the first row.

11. And the second row, an emerald, a sapphire, and a diamond.

12. And the third row, a ligure, an agate, and an amethyst.

13. And the fourth row, a beryl, an onyx, and a jasper: they were inclosed in ouches of gold in their inclosings.

14. And the stones were according to the names of the children of Israel, twelve, according to their names, like the engravings of a signet, every one with his name, according to the twelve tribes.

15. And they made upon the breastplate, chains at the ends, of wreathen work of pure gold.

16. And they made two ouches of gold, and two gold rings; and put the two rings in the two ends of the breastplate.

17. And they put the two wreathen chains of gold in the two rings on the ends of the breastplate.

18. And the two ends of the two wreathen chains they fastened in the two ouches, and put them on the shoulderpieces of the ephod, before it.

19. And they made two rings of gold, and put them on the two ends of the breastplate, upon the border of it, which was on the side of the ephod inward.

The *Porter Rhodes* diamond was exhibited in 1880 and the publicity given to this stone, together with the interest shown in it by Queen Victoria and Empress

Eugénie, helped dispel the myth that South African diamonds were inferior to those from India and Brazil.[1]

The *Southern Cross* was exhibited in 1886. It consists of a cluster of nine pearls naturally formed into a cross and measures 37.2 mm by 18.3 mm. The Cross was discovered in 1883 by a boy, Tom Clarke, in Baldwin Creek while fishing from 'Shiner' Kelly's schooner, 'Ethel'. When Clarke removed it from the shell it broke into three pieces. Kelly, when he first saw the configuration, was unimpressed and dropped it into a pickle bottle. He later sold it to a fellow pearler, Frank Roy, for £10 and a bottle of rum. Roy sold it on to a Cossack publican, Frank Craig, for £40. Craig had the pearl doctor, Horrie Sholl, work on it, who joined the pieces together and put them into an expensive setting. Craig formed a syndicate and exhibited the Cross in Europe.

However, Henry Taunton, an English adventurer and writer, states in his book *Australind,* that the Cross is a fake. He claims that when he saw it in 1883, it was in three pieces and that the Cross had no left arm. He maintained that another pearl was found to finish the Cross.

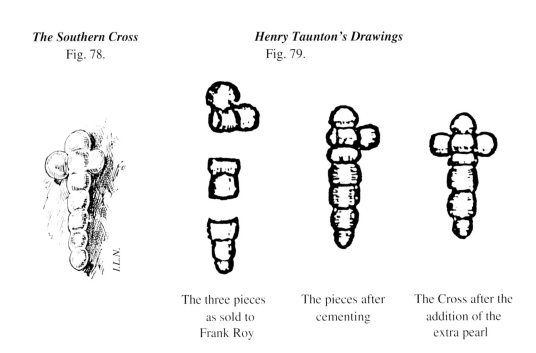

The Southern Cross   **Henry Taunton's Drawings**
Fig. 78.   Fig. 79.

The three pieces   The pieces after   The Cross after the
as sold to   cementing   addition of the
Frank Roy   extra pearl

In 1924 it was bought by C. Peto Bennett of Lombard Street and valued at £24,000.

---

1 See Balfour, p.140.

English Roman Catholics were reputed to have organised a collection to purchase the Cross and present it to the Pope but Taburiaux[1] states that it now belongs to an Australian syndicate. In 1981 it was shown to Christie's with a view to a possible sale. They had it tested by the Gem Testing Laboratory of Great Britain who wrote up their findings in their Journal of July 1986. It was concluded that the piece may be unsound and the sale did not go ahead.

Streeter's staple clientele were the rising Victorian middle class. He must have gone for high turnover but he did not ignore the top end of the market and some spectacular pieces and stones were to pass through his doors.

In 1875 he was admitted, by redemption, to the Freedom of the Clockmakers' Company. Four years later he also joined the Gold and Silver Wyre Drawers' Company and was to serve on their Court of Assistants. In the year of joining he presented the Clockmakers with a collection of one chronometer and 14 movements. The donations were described in the 1902 catalogue of the Clockmakers' Company thus:

ANON

19. Movement - Vertical; enamel dial, not original, both hands wanting. The movement is a very thick one and the engraving of the balance-cock and the slide are of a bold design, originally well-executed and gilt, but altered by some subsequent treatment. Early 18th century.

ANTES, John

34. Chronometer - Pair-case pocket-chronometer; inner and outer cases silver; enamel dial, with seconds. The balance is a plain one of steel and of rather large size. The pendulum-spring very small, and almost hidden by the balance-cock, upon which is the regulating work. Date of hallmark, 1787-8.

John Antes, London

BARON, Jean

47. Movement - Vertical; enamel dial. Early 18th century.

Jean Baron, Utrecht

CABRIER, Charles

81. Movement - Vertical; enamel dial, hands wanting. Peculiar vase-shaped, fluted pillars. Early 18th century.

C. Cabrier, London 1908

---

1 *Pearls* by Jean Taburiaux. N.A.G. Press, 1985.

DECHARMES, Simon

98. Movement - Vertical; dial wanting. Pierced tulip pillars. Early 18th century.

S. Decharmes, London

FROMANTEEL

127.   Movement - Vertical; dial and minute-hand wanting. Originally made for one hand only, it has since had motion-work added to carry a pair of hands. Tulip pillars. This is probably a very early conversion.

Fromanteel [1]

GIB, William

129.   Movement - Vertical; enamel dial, both hands wanting. An old 'pendule' movement, the balance so constructed as to give it the appearance of a pendulum. Early 18th century.

William Gib, Rotterdam, 1653

HIGGS AND EVANS

179.   Movement - Vertical; enamel dial of later date. Remarkable for the unique character of its pillars. End of 18th century.

Higgs & Evans, London, 6314

HOCKER, John

180.   Movement - Vertical; enamel dial. About 1730.

John Hocker, Reading [2]

LAINY, David

200.   Movement - Vertical; enamel dial, not original, minute-hand wanting. Of an early period, and remarkable for the peculiar cutting of its tulip pillars and the mode of fixing in case, the balance-cock and other pierced and chased parts on the top plate. About 1680-90.

David Lainy

NERRY, John

240.   Movement - Vertical; dial wanting. In imperfect state; curiously shaped pillars. Middle of 18th century.

Jn. Nerry, London 233

---

1 Probably the work of Ahasuerus Fromanteel the Elder, Freeman, 23 November 1632, but others of this family were members of the trade and connected with the Company, *inter* 1655-1680.

2 A John Hocker was admitted Freeman, 19 January 1729.

ORDSON, William

245.   Movement - Vertical; enamel dial. For the usual hour-numerals are substituted the letters of the name 'James Newman' and an asterisk. Square pillars. Early 18th century.

Wm. Ordson, London, 8418

RENSMAN, Gerrit

258.   Movement - Vertical; enamel dial. Very fine pillars. Early 18th century.

Gerrit Rensman, Zwol

SWAAN, Pieter

279.   Movement - Vertical; enamel dial, both hands wanting. An ancient movement with elaborate pillars, chased and engraved. It is much worn. End of 17th century.

Pieter Swaan, Amsterdam, 620

TOMPION, Thomas

288.   Movement - Vertical; dial wanting. End of 17th or early 18th century.

Tho. Tompion, London, 2268

The only items which survive from this donation are the movement by Fromanteel (Fig. 80) and the chronometer by John Antes (Figs. 81 and 82).

Fig. 80. The movement by Fromanteel

Fig. 81. The Chronometer by John Antes

Fig. 82. The Chronometer open showing the labels of various repairers.

It is astounding to record that from this donation of fifteen pieces, the Worshipful Company have managed to retain only two, the chronometer by John Antes and the movement by Fromanteel. They have lost seven pieces and sold six; the Baron, Hocker, Lainy, Nerry, Rensman and Tompion. This sale was held at Sotheby's in 1981, ostensibly to dispose of duplicates. Sir George White, the current keeper of the collection, has commented that, in the light of his recent research, the sale was infinitely regrettable as many of the items sold had important associations and were central to the history of the Collection. The Court of 1981 took the decision to sell and chose the particular items. In the annals of custodianship, the name of the Clockmakers does not shine brightly. It is worth noting that Streeter never joined the Goldsmiths' Company although he had harmonious relations with them over the years and regarded them as Fathers of the Trade. Probably this Company was too exclusive for a relative newcomer.[1]

In 1874 the Ladies of Chislehurst commissioned from Streeter, a 'Coming of Age' gift for their neighbour, the Prince Imperial. He was the son of Emperor Napoleon II, who had sought exile in England after his defeat in the Franco-Prussian wars. Known as the *Prince Imperial Inkstand,* it was in the form of a beehive with symbolic Imperial bees resting on the hive. On the summit is the national eagle. The rest has the tricolour in relief and the front has the jewelled monogram *L.N.* in sapphires, diamonds and rubies. Around the base are oriental amethysts representing the imperial colour set in gold. The gift sadly did not bring the Prince any luck. He was to die five years later seeking to prove himself in the Zulu Wars whilst in charge of Streeter's fellow company director, Lord Chelmsford.

Edwin has a special section in his catalogue on Presentation Plate. He stated:

As it is almost always imperative in the case of Presentation Plate, that the article or piece should partake of the character of the occasion, it is impossible to give many illustrations in a catalogue.

Mr. Streeter has therefore made the most complete arrangements for the preparation of any designs or drawings by the most skilful artists, which can be supplied at very short notice, if particulars and full requirements are sent.

---

1 His son, Harry Edwin, was apprenticed in 1875 to the Goldsmith, Thomas Eady of 26 Red Lion Street, Clerkenwell. He died before he could become a Freeman. Another son, George, was apprenticed to his father as a clockmaker in 1879 but never graduated to Freemanship.

Fig. 83. The Prince Imperial Inkstand

Presentation Plate.
Fig. 84. The Regimental Mess Centre Piece of the 38th Regiment

In cases of larger pieces of Plate for Regimental Messes, etc, a full-sized Model in addition to drawings can be prepared, so as to form a better estimate of the piece required.

In all presentations, Mr Streeter, will be glad to make special terms as to reduction of price, taking into consideration the advantage derived from the publicity.

An interesting presentation piece was a silver model of Fort Valerien, Paris, commissioned by the *Daily News* and presented to the besieged residents whose letters were published in that paper. Another was the Regimental Mess Centre Piece for the 38th Regiment - now the Staffordshire Regiment - described as being between three and four feet high, a classical shaped vase with shields, in repoussé work, of Lucknow and Sevastopol; the case is supported by a square base, on the corners of which are mounted, in silver, finely modelled figures, representing the four Continents; between the figures are richly chased subjects of the most important engagements in which this well-known Regiment has taken prominent part.

The picture below illustrates a Presentation Clock for the 42nd Highlanders (now the Black Watch). It was presented in 1867 by Captain, the Hon. R. H. Stewart in remembrance of twelve years' service in the Crimea, England and India.

Black Watch

Fig. 85. The Presentation Clock for the 42nd Highlanders

In 1877 Streeter published his first full length book, *Precious Stones and Gems.* This book built on a similar one, *Diamonds and Precious Stones,* written ten years earlier by his former employer, Harry Emanuel. The book sold well and ran into six editions, the last one being published in 1898. As Streeter expanded and improved his book through the editions, he found it necessary to write separate books on certain topics so *Great Diamonds of the World* was issued in 1882, going to two editions. *Pearls and Pearling Life* came out in 1886. These books, today, are most readable and are often quoted by current writers.

Edwin devised a novel way of having his proofs read. He sent the manuscript of the section of his book on the *Koh-i-noor* to Queen Victoria and she graciously approved. The sections on the *Pitt* and *Eugénie* diamonds he sent to Empress Eugénie of France, who added some notes. These two articles were reprinted in a small presentation volume to celebrate Victoria's Diamond Jubilee.

However, the books do contain a number of contradictions and disproved theories. The most glaring contradiction concerns the *Koh-i-noor* and *Great Mogul* diamonds. In one edition the author emphatically states that they are the same stone and in a later one, equally emphatically, he states that they are different. But it must be remembered that the history of ancient diamonds involves building up a story from incomplete evidence and separating myth from fact. It is quite reasonable to revise theories in the light of new findings and opinions.

As John Culme points out in his *Directory of Silversmiths,* the careers of Emanuel and Streeter have a number of parallels. They both took over businesses that had been bankrupt. They both wrote books, were good self-publicists, and both financed disastrous geological expeditions to South Africa. They were, however, of differing religions and Streeter did not launch into a second career of European aristocrat and Central American Ambassador.

Increasing prosperity allowed Streeter to take a country house, Callis Court, at St. Peter's in Kent. He also moved with his growing family, shortly to be nine children, into The Mount, 4 Primrose Hill Road. By 1880 there was an office in Ceylon. Ferguson's *1883/4 Ceylon Directory* lists E. W. Streeter, Jeweller, 10 Prince Street, The Fort, Colombo with James Hagerand, Agent and F. Thornton, Assistant.

In 1880 the pearl fishings in Ceylon were reopened. There is a lively account of Streeter's agent's involvement in *Pearls and Pearling Life* and one can do no better than reprint the story.

AUCTION OF PEARL OYSTERS IN CEYLON.

Fig. 86.

After a number of unsuccessful Pearl Fisheries, the attention of the Ceylon Government was called to the considerable decrease in the revenue, arising from this particular department, and a special officer was appointed to inspect the banks periodically, and report upon the condition of the various beds. A most able and zealous officer was appointed - namely, Captain Donnan, the master-attendant of the harbour of Colombo. This gentleman made frequent surveys, and at proper periods he employed, for temporary purposes, certain divers, who brought up samples of the oysters. These oysters were carefully washed, and the Pearls found were catalogued, so as to arrive at an average result in preparing for a more extensive fishery. In the year 1879, such a preliminary fishery had been attempted, and in consequence of the general good average of the yield of Pearls, the Ceylon Government decided to organise the following year a much more extensive fishery, so as to embrace a large number of previously explored banks, which had been reported as having yielded a high percentage of fine Pearls.

The usual notices were circulated throughout Ceylon and India, and created considerable excitement amongst the natives, as for many years the fisheries had yielded such poor results that Pearls were becoming exceedingly scarce, as indeed they still are.

Previously to this fishery, no European had ever ventured upon the speculation of buying oysters on a large scale; although for many years, as each successive fishery had been conducted by the government, a few Europeans, such as the military officers and merchants of Ceylon, had speculated in a small number of oysters, to the extent of £2 or £3, just as they might venture on a Derby sweepstake. But no regular organised washing of Pearl oysters had ever been attempted by any European. The whole business had for generations been monopolised by the native merchants from the bazaars of India and Ceylon.

The report of the survey being encouraging, and the sample of Pearls found in the preliminary diving having been above the average, both in yield and in quality, the author of this work determined upon speculating, and accordingly, an agent was commissioned in Colombo to attend the public auction, and bid for the whole of the yield of the fisheries. But the Ceylon Government refused to entertain any single private offer or tender, and determined to put the oysters up in lots in the usual way.

The fisheries were held off the N.W. coast of Ceylon, at a district called Silavatorrai, or Silvatura, a most inaccessible place, the only means of transport being by common fishing canoes, or by chartering a special steamer.

The fleet consisted of two divisions alternately working the banks, which were situated at a distance of about ten to fifteen miles from the shore. The agent had arranged for native brokers to purchase at market rates as many lots as possible, and the prices varied each day, according to the reports of successful finding of Pearls. In rough numbers, a quarter of a million of oysters were purchased. As the distance from Silavatorrai to Colombo was not only very great, but bare of all means of transport, a fleet of boats was kept constantly employed in sailing between the fishery station and Colombo, until all the oysters purchased had been brought to the capital.

The preparation of a place to receive the oysters, and to carry on the washing and search for Pearls, proved a most difficult undertaking. The first journey of the small fleet landed about 12,000 oysters, each boat capable of carrying a thousand. The sacks containing the oysters were sealed at Silavatorrai, whilst the oysters were alive, and were conveyed to a large building on the beach at Colombo. Preparations were at once made for immediate washing, but unfortunately the difficult passage from Silavatorrai to Colombo, with contrary winds, had so delayed the arrival of the boats, that by the time they had reached the capital, the sacks of oysters emitted a most unpleasant odour. The Superintendant of Police, Captain Hansard, upon receiving a complaint from the residents in the neighbourhood, at once communicated with the agent, and threatened confiscation of the whole cargo, if not immediately removed. On receipt of this communication from the police, the agent immediately prepared four large tin-lined cases, in which were packed a sample of 10,000 oysters. These were to be shipped at once to England, in order to ascertain by personal knowledge, the most satisfactory method of securing the Pearls. It was intended that the washing should take place at Buxted, on the river Ouse, near the Crowborough Hills, in Sussex, where plenty of running water could be obtained for the purpose.

In the meantime the boats had been arriving at Colombo with fresh lots of oysters, and it became imperatively necessary to provide a suitable place wherein to warehouse them, especially as they were fast decomposing. A second place was therefore engaged, about nine miles from Colombo, in a very sparsely-populated native village. Here, whilst erecting temporary huts and buildings for warehousing the oysters, and making the necessary arrangements for washing them, a second notice from the police arrived, forbidding any attempt to commence operations. The inhabitants refused to allow the erection of buildings to proceed, and after considerable delay, the authorities suggested a district several miles away from the village, in the Ratnapura Road. By bribing the few inhabitants who were within a mile of the locality, permission was at last given to conduct the washing at this spot.

By this time the accumulation of several boat-loads was causing considerable indignation in Colombo, and a general protest was being made against the offending oysters. It must be admitted that there was ample cause for this interference, inasmuch as the horrible odour threatened some fearful plague. As speedily therefore as possible - bullock carts being the only available means of transport - the oysters were packed and despatched under guard, to the place appointed, and a large native hut was hired in the neighbourhood where the sacks were deposited as the different cartloads arrived. To make this hut more secure, it was boarded up with planks, and every means of entry stopped, except a door, which was protected by stout padlocks. At special request, the authorities had arranged for private duty four policemen, who in turns guarded the hut and its valuable contents, by night and day for a month.

Much preparation of the ground had to be made, and hence there was necessarily some delay before operations could be commenced. A deep cutting in connection with a neighbouring stream had to be effected, in order to get a continuous flow of water. The staff numbered about forty, including four native inspectors, selected from the moormen community, who represent almost exclusively the previous stone and gem merchants of Ceylon. The rest consisted of coolie labourers, both Tamil and Cingalese, who were to work and search for the hidden Pearls.

It may occur to certain persons that the washing of the oyster is an easy task, and the subsequent finding - or chance of finding - a valuable Pearl, is sufficient reward for the labour. Possibly it may sometimes be so, but in this case matters were entirely different, for the oysters had arrived at such a state of decomposition that they had generated small larvae in such incredible quantities, that only natives of the lowest caste could be induced to enter the hut. When the sacks were brought into the open, the contents were emptied into large barrels or tubs; when these were about half full of oysters, the water was turned on and flowed in continuously. Around each tub four coolies were stationed, each under the inspector, and as each oyster was fished up the shell was washed clean, and if it contained no Pearl, was thrown on one side.

As a rule the larger Pearls were invariably found in the hinge of the oyster, ofter imbedded in the decayed matter, and required some effort to dislodge them. In a few instances they were slightly adhering to the shell and almost required cutting away, but as a rule, the Pearl was so loosely fixed in the oyster itself, that it fell out readily as the mollusc was washed. The greater number of Pearls, however, were discovered at the bottom of the tub, mixed with shining portions of broken shell. As fast as each lot was inspected, the Pearls that were found were bottled and carefully sealed preparatory to their final washing and cleaning in rice, which effectually prepared them for the London Market.

During the time of washing, large bonfires were kept continually burning; but notwithstanding all precautions it was impossible to prevent disastrous effects on some of the men employed, especially the Europeans: the coolies alone seemed able to endure the horrible surroundings.

Every possible care was, of course, taken to guard against robbery. Orders had been issued that every man engaged in the washing was to be stripped, with the exception of the scantiest loin cloth. Moreover, the chewing of betel and other masticatories commonly used by the natives was prohibited while they were at this work, for it is not an uncommon thing, when such orders are not insisted upon, that under the pretence of chewing the betel, they adroitly slip into the mouth any rare Pearl, and effectually hide it from the owner; indeed, cases have been known in which the more adventurous have swallowed several Pearls. However, such precautions were taken that the chance of their so cunningly disposing of the gems could only occur on any occasional absence or slight inattention of the overseers.

Considering the magnitude of the undertaking, it was impossible to entirely control the thievish propensities of the native coolies, who have a very low standard of morality. Robbery is considered by no means a disgrace, or even a wrong, unless detected. Nevertheless, a satisfactory result was obtained as regards the actual net receipt of Pearls. It is true that not many large or fine gems were found, but the quantity of small ordinary Pearls was very good, and reached a total of some thousands of grains. The largest Pearls, which attained an average weight of about nine or ten grains each, were very round and well-shaped, but unfortunately were not of the best colour.

The most unfortunate condition of the Pearl fishery was the avarice of the Government, who in order to secure an increase to their yearly revenue, had opened the fishery before the oysters were of mature age. The result of this short sightedness was that the Pearls found were of smaller size and less in number than would probably have been the case had the fishery been longer delayed. Of this there was unmistakable proof in the opinion of native experts, inasmuch as very many of the shells contained large unformed Pearls, which, if longer time had been given, would probably have developed into valuable and perfect gems, but which in their immature state were useless. Some two or three hundred of these shells had as many as from twenty to thirty massed together, but most of these were imperfectly formed and useless for ornamentation.

It is held by some authorities that when oysters are left in a decaying condition, the skin of the Pearl is seriously impaired. This is so in the Australian fisheries, but was certainly not the case in Ceylon, for experience has shewn that equally good Pearls have been found in the shells which have been immediately washed while the oyster is alive, and in those which have been buried for weeks, and generated larvae.

Whilst the early washing of the oysters just described was proceeding, the four cases already mentioned, containing several thousand of originally sealed sacks from Silavatorrai, had been shipped by the W.W.Co to the harbour for putting on board the steamer in order to be forwarded for examination to the author in London; but owing to a few days' delay, decomposition proceeded so rapidly, that a foul gas was generated, which burst open the tin-lined cases, and polluted the atmosphere for miles around. The inhabitants of the Fort district of Colombo naturally complained to the authorities, who thereupon seized the cases, and threatened confiscation if they were not immediately removed. But the difficulty was to dispose of them, as no place could be found in which the authorities would permit them to be buried. Ultimately they were taken in bullock-carts to the bungalow of the agent, who had been sent for in haste from the scene of the washing operations, and he at once had pits dug to receive them. In support of the view that decaying matter does not injure the Pearl, the fact may be stated that two months afterwards the pits were opened, and Pearls were found equal in quality to those which the earlier and less polluted oyster had yielded.

In all the more recent fisheries, great competition has existed between local Ceylon native dealers, chetties, and others who come over from India, more especially from Madras and Bombay. As a consequence of such competition, the price has risen considerably for the oyster, although the yield of the oyster in fine Pearls, has been less. Formerly at the public auction, 15 rupees was a fair average price for a thousand oysters, but in the fishery of 1880, the competition was so keen that several lots reached 60 and 70 rupees a thousand. To this must be added the great expense of transfer to Colombo, and the many changes necessary before the final washing was undertaken; considering the uncertain chances of the yield of Pearls, the speculation becomes as risky as a gambling table.

No doubt if the business were conducted entirely by natives, much of the expense could be saved, as the Pearls might then be washed at the fishing station; but from the intense heat and discomfort of a tropical country, residence in a temporary hut and exposure for weeks to a dangerous atmosphere, scarcely any European could live there, and, indeed, very few of the natives cared to undertake operations on the spot. The enterprise is a most speculative one, and is scarcely ever found to be a profitable transaction, even when pursued entirely by the natives.

For the purchaser of oysters a much safer and more lucrative result could be obtained by purchasing of the small dealers, the little lots of Pearls that each derives from his oysters. This has been proved by personal experience. The government agent, in payment of the boatmen and divers who engage in the fishery, allots one fourth of the yield of each boatful of oysters to them; and these lots are allowed to be put up separately, and in many cases are sold in small and convenient quantities to suit all purchasers.

In some instances the boatmen wash the oysters themselves, but in either case, a good judge of Pearls can, with much greater safety, buy the gems themselves rather than venture upon large quantities of oysters, with their attendant trouble and expense, and the chance of perhaps, after all, realizing an insufficient quantity of Pearls to reimburse him for the outlay.

Most of the Pearls from these fisheries are secured by the Indian chetties, as Bombay is considered a much better market for them than Ceylon or even London; much higher prices are paid by the wealthy Rajahs of India direct to the Pearl merchants, than could ever be got from London dealers. Notwithstanding the frequent fisheries and finds of Pearls, it is nearly impossible to buy any really fine ones in Ceylon.

Immediately after the famous Pearl fishery of 1880, scarcely a Pearl of any size or value was to be obtained in Colombo. Several orders were received by the agent from persons who were unable to buy oysters, or who had been unsuccessful in finding Pearls. As these orders could not be executed there, the Pearls were procured from the London market. Some of the wealthy natives, resident in Ceylon, succeeded in collecting a few Pearls of fair size and value, but only for a very limited number; indeed, as a depot for Pearls, Ceylon was as inferior in supply a month after the fishery, as any small provincial town in England could have been. It may be confidently asserted that if the Pearls which had been sent to London had been kept in Ceylon, and sold when the excitement and demand were at their height, far higher prices would have been realized.

Buxted in Sussex is referred to in this account, where Streeter was to purchase a small estate, Sackville Place, and he had a country home in the village until his retirement in 1905. It is not known what the good folk of Sussex would have made of quarter of a million putrescent oysters, the stench of which was too strong even for the hardened Ceylonese native.

The history of Sackville Place, or, as it is now called, Olive House, is interesting and worth recalling in detail. The original house, at first called New House Farm, was of some antiquity. It and the surrounding estate were once owned by the Alchorne family who can trace their roots back to the twelfth century. S. H. Grimm drew the house in watercolour and ink in 1780 (Fig. 87). A connection with the Olive family is indicated by a rebus of an olive at the top of the front gate. A tile now fixed to the stable wall bears the inscription 'John Olive made these 1741'.

Fig. 87. S. H. Grimm's watercolour and ink drawing of New Home Farm dated 1780

Fig. 88. The House, now renamed Sackville Place, in 1880 after alterations

In the seventeenth century the surrounding lands belonged to Dr. Anthony Saunders, Rector of Buxted, Vicar of Acton and a treasurer of St Paul's Cathedral. He founded Uckfield Grammar School and he bequeathed the estate to a trust for the education of twelve boys of Buxted and Uckfield. Writing scratched in a pane in a rear ground window reads 'John Olive July 16 1819'.

Kelly's Directory of 1862 records Edward Olive, Farmer, as resident, presumably as tenant or lessee. The estate came up for sale by auction on 11 August 1880 under the hammer of Sainsbury Gilbert & Co. of Old Jewry Chambers. Edwin Streeter bought the freehold and leasehold interests but he must have been involved earlier because plans exist, drawn up by the architect William Allport dated 2 May 1872, for the conversion of the old two storey farm house into a modern Victorian residence, with three stories and attic. The Olive family were still involved at this stage because there is reference on the plans to a sworn affidavit in the matter of John Olive, a person of unsound mind. Perhaps this lunatic held a leasehold interest. The plans were implemented and the prose of the agents in the 1880 catalogue matches well with current estate agents' hyperbole. The catalogue reads:

The Sackville House Estate

of
447 acres
on the
Southern slope of Crowborough Plateau
'Queen Anne' Residence upon which £5,000 has recently been spent in rendering
it in every detail of taste and luxury one of the most
enjoyable residences in Sussex
with
Beautiful Pleasure Grounds
Excellent farm buildings
thriving and heavily-timbered woods
well watered with
miles of trout stream and fishing
a pleasure farm of 45 acres
three residences or hunting boxes and several cottages
Running through the centre of the estate is a curious
RIDGE OF ROCKS, similar but superior to the High Rocks
at Tunbridge Wells which here forms a
beautiful natural terrace known as the Vineyard Route
and hermitage
Traces of there having been a Vineyard still remain;
also a curious rock habitation comprising three large
living rooms hewn in solid rock

With its new found status the house had been renamed Sackville House, Sackville being the family name of the Earls de la Warr who were Lords of the Manor.

Edwin had the house as his country residence until the turn of the century. However, by 1903 *Kelly's* lists him still as one of the principal landowners in the village but residing at 'The Primroses', a smaller house on the estate. Perhaps the lease had run out, and with his family having grown up, he chose a smaller dwelling. Martin Bros., dairymen, are listed at New House Farm, the building having reverted to its earlier name.

The estate must have been sold around 1905, at the time of Edwin's financial embarrassment and retirement. Fergus Bowes-Lyon, the fourth brother of the Queen Mother, lived there before the First World War. While serving as a Captain in the Black Watch, he was killed at the Battle of Loos in 1915, aged 26, leaving one daughter.

After the war the house reverted to a farmhouse and in 1938, R.E. Preston & Sons, farmers, are listed.

Around the time of the Second World War, the house and farm were bought by a Mr. Fegan. He started a children's home and the property became known as Fegan's Farm and Fegan's Home. The home was highly religious and the children made to work on the farm so as to make the venture pay. Subsequently, those running the home indulged in such fanatical activities that the authorities had to take action.

Later the entire estate, the house now called Olive House, was bought by John Platts-Mills, Q.C., Labour M.P. for Finsbury from 1945 to 1950 and Defence Counsel for the Kray brothers. The current freeholders are Ian and Susan Daniel, to whom I am very grateful for much of the information included here.

A particularly interesting feature of the estate is the Hermitage Rocks. A good description of these and the remains of the vineyard is found in the *Uckfield Visitor's Guide* published *c.*1870.

An archaeological excavation of the Rocks was written up in *Sussex Archaeological Collections 119 (1981) 1-36* under the title *A Late Mesolithic Rock-Shelter Site at High Hurstwood, Sussex* by R.M. Jacobi and C.F.Tebbutt.

Charles Dawson, the central figure in the Piltdown Man hoax, also wrote a short history of the Hermitage.[1] He recounts that while a new house was being built by E.W. Streeter as an estate improvement, a large grave was discovered, cut into the sand at the top of the rock, containing a human skeleton. There was speculation that this may have been the hermit who carved the Rock.

---

1 *History of the Hermitage at Buxted, Sussex* by Chas. Dawson, Uckfield, n.d. Only known copy in Lewes Library.

CHAPTER FOUR

PEARLS AND PEARLING LIFE

It is not known when Streeter initiated his pearling expeditions, but by around 1881 he had purchased from the Rajah of Pas Sair in Singapore, the *Sree Pas-Sair,* a 112-ton brigantine. The name means *The Belle of Pas Sair*, a district of Borneo, and she carried eight dinghies and held sufficient water for 80 men for three months. The Captain of the vessel was E.C. Chippindall, late of the Royal Navy.

Edward Cockayne Chippindall was a younger son of the Revd. John Chippindall, M.A., Rector of St. Luke's, Cheetham, Manchester. Born in 1852, he enlisted as a midshipman in the Royal Navy in 1866, serving on the *H.M.S. Eclipse*. He became a Sub-Lieutenant in 1871 but, finding the pay insufficient, commuted his commission and joined the Merchant Navy, serving as First Officer on S.S. *Calabar*. This ship came to grief, so in 1875, he purchased a plantation on Fiji. According to his father, this project prospered. He 'turned a wilderness into an Eden' and employed up to 100 men. Controversy arose when he crossed the path of Sir Arthur Gordon, Governor of Fiji, later first Lord Stanmore and son of the Victorian Prime Minister, the Earl of Aberdeen. Chippindall's view of the story is recorded in an open letter from his father to the Earl of Kimberley, the Colonial Secretary. The letter was published as a pamphlet and sold for one penny. A copy is in the British Museum. Edward was arrested on a charge of the wilful murder of a native, his horse-boy 'Jacky'. The Revd. Chippindall relays the story as follows:

Jacky was engaged, under my son's direction, in driving a horse attached to a tram-cart which was then being used in bringing the sugar-cane to the mill. Thinking him rather clumsy and slow, and not knowing that the boy at the moment was feeling ill, my son, who was then wearing, as was his invariable habit when superintending his men, a pair of thin canvas slippers with india rubber soles, touched him with his foot, playfully adding, 'Come, Jacky, be quick'. The boy at once quickened his pace, took the loaded cart to the mill, unloaded it there, and returning, worked as usual that day and the day following, when he was obliged to discontinue work, owing to what my son thought was a slight bilious attack. The boy was given some medicine, but, complaining of pain in the stomach and chest and under the arms, my son sent him into hospital, assigned him a nurse, and asked Dr. Farquharson, the resident medical man, to attend him. Dr. Farquharson made a most careful examination of the case, stripped him entirely of any little clothing he wore, and is ready to swear that when he examined him, viz., two days after these facts which I have related, there was neither bruise nor wound of any kind upon any portion of his body, but that, in his opinion, the boy was suffering from disease of the lungs.

My son was at the time confined to his room with sickness, but sent down from his own table every delicacy he could provide, and heard from his manager, Mr. Wiseman, daily accounts of the boy's health. During his illness he frequently expressed to those about him, his gratitude to his master for all his kindness, and especially while he was sick, and in the presence of others declared he was dying of the 'big sickness', which he said he had caught in the neighbouring town. The boy died, to my son's regret, and nothing more was heard of the circumstance till three weeks after, when my son perceived three persons, apparently strangers, coming along his tramway and approaching his house. He at once went out to welcome, with the hospitality to which many can bear testimony, and found them to be - (1) Dr. Cruikshank, Assistant Medical Officer; (2) the Inspector of Immigrants; (3) a Police Officer. Dr. Cruikshank then addressed him thus: 'Mr. Chippindall, we are come upon a most painful errand, viz., to arrest you as having caused the death of one of your servants.' 'Good God' my son exclaimed, in indignant horror, 'How?' He was answered - 'By brutally kicking him to death.'

Dr. Cruikshank then, under my son's directions, had the body exhumed, and after the most careful examination declared that the accusation, in his opinion, was utterly false, - that there was not the slightest evidence of violence, but that from the state of the lungs he was convinced that death had been caused by pneumonia. He then warmly congratulated my son, who, however, declined to accept the congratulations, and inquired further on whose evidence such a charge had been made. It then transpired that certain Mallicolo men, - cannibals, and of the lowest type, - men who have no notion of truth, and in whose minds human life is appraised no higher than that of a pig, had laid this accusation against a master who had always treated them and all others with uniform kindness, but against whom they bore the following grudge:-

These men had been engaged for three years' service, and of this, two-and-a-half had expired. Ignorant, however, of the lapse of time, they imagined that they were being kept beyond their engagement, and declared that 'they would get the master into trouble somehow or other.' These men were heard by others whose evidence will be given upon the trial, concocting a conspiracy and declaring that they would accuse my son of causing Jacky's death, while at the same time they endeavoured to spread disaffection among the others, whom ineffectually they tried to persuade to join them. This will explain the motive of the charge.

After his examination of the body, Dr. Cruikshank, the Inspector of Immigrants, and the Police Officer, went to my son's house, and having been hospitably entertained, left the plantation, and the whole affair was supposed to be at an end. That night, however, (April 29), at 10.30, the Police Officer returned, and in the face of the report given by the Medical Officer (Dr. Cruikshank), arrested my son upon the charge of wilful murder with 'malice prepense' etc. All his property in the house was then overhauled, in order to find the 'iron boot' which his accusers declared had been the cause of Jacky's death. My son invited inspection, threw open every door and box, but nothing was found bearing upon the case except one boot, perfectly clean, and which can be proved by his servants to have been never used since the making of a molasses tank, which had been completed long before.

The Police Officer who thus arrested my son was not at the time in possession of a warrant, at least so I gather from my son's letter. It had been applied for, but had been refused by the Magistrate, Mr. Anson, in consequence of the testimony of Dr. Cruikshank, who had wholly exculpated my son from all complicity in the charge. The Police Officer acted with great personal propriety, and frequently expressed his deep regret, - not because he was at the time acting without a warrant, but because he was obliged, as he believed, to act thus against a man for whom he entertained so sincere a respect. My son acknowledged his courtesy, overlooked all informalities, and voluntarily placed himself in his hands.

He was then ignominiously taken in company with a friend, a Mr. Haynes, who was at the time his guest, to the Court House, three miles distant, and there found that Sir Arthur Gordon had sent from Levuka, the Crown Prosecutor, with instructions 'to prosecute in any case.' These instructions were then literally acted upon, and the medical testimony of Dr. Cruikshank, to the effect that death had been caused only by pneumonia, was ignored, and my son found himself, for the first time in his life, arraigned before a court in which the Prosecutor was apparently all-powerful, and the prisoner was alone and undefended. No time was given him to prepare his case, - no information was supplied as to the evidence. There he stood, the victim of a Crown prosecution, with no one to speak for him, and unable, by the rules of the Court, to give evidence for himself. The witnesses were then called, not one by one, but were brought into Court in a mass, and openly directed as to the evidence they should give by the Crown Prosecutor, who instructed them on the importance of all telling the same tale, and swearing to the same facts. My son remonstrated upon the unfairness of such proceedings, whereupon these witnesses were removed into an adjoining room, in which, however, they were still able to confer together and agree upon what to say. Notwithstanding these facilities given, their evidence totally disagreed, both as to the facts themselves and the locality where the supposed crime was perpetrated. Upon my son pointing out these discrepancies, the Crown Prosecutor exclaimed, - 'What are you trying to prove? Everybody knows these men are only telling lies.'

The Court then broke up at a late hour, the Magistrate went to his own house accompanied by the Police Officer, while my son and the rest slept at the Court House. About two o'clock in the morning, my son, who was fast asleep at the time, was awakened by someone pulling him by the arm; it was Mr. Anson, the Magistrate, who took him outside and said, - 'I cannot bear to let you remain feeling that such a charge is hanging over your head, and knowing you to be absolutely innocent.' He then added, 'You are released from the charge. I have already written my judgement, and tomorrow morning, in the presence of everyone, white and black, I shall publicly dismiss the case.'

Next morning (May 1), the Court re-opened, when my son expected that the Magistrate would fulfil his promise. To his indignant surprise, the Crown Prosecutor refused to accept the decision of the Magistrate, saying that he had written instructions from Sir Arthur Gordon, backed by much stronger verbal directions, to prosecute my son 'under any circumstances whatever.' More witness of the same character were then produced, and at 6.15 pm the case for the Prosecution closed.

My son then, wholly undefended and alone, insisted upon the production of the medical testimony of Dr. Cruikshank and Dr. Farquharson; but, finding all he could say of little avail, he declared his purpose of reserving his defence. One concession to his innocence was indeed made. The charge was changed from one of wilful murder to manslaughter; and heavy bail being accepted, my son was permitted to return to his estate.

Thus closed a preliminary trial, which is a disgrace only to the prosecution.

The letter is a plea for an inquiry into the conduct of Sir Arthur Gordon and the Revd. Chippindall concludes it with the good news that he has just received a telegram reporting that a full and honourable acquittal had been announced. Questions were asked in the House of Commons of the Minister concerned, M.E.Grant Duff, M.P., and Sir Arthur records his aspect of the story in his printed papers, also to be found in the British Museum. He states that, 'there is not a page - I might almost say not a line - of the pamphlet that does not contain false or erroneous statements.' He comments, 'I have had literally nothing to do with the case, and there is consequently no 'conduct' of mine concerning it into which to enquire.' On his transfer to become Governor of New Zealand, Sir Arthur gave an address to the islanders where he summed up the case thus:

Information, supported by a large mass of evidence, is received by the police to the effect that a labourer has received from his employer, injuries, of the effects of which he died, and that the dead man has been buried surreptitiously and without the report required by law. The police, as is their clear duty, lay this information before the Stipendiary Magistrate. The Magistrate, after hearing the evidence, commits the accused for trial, as on the evidence before him, he was manifestly bound to do. On the trial, the accused is acquitted. Meanwhile, the greatest indignation is expressed at the committal on such a charge of a member of the 'dominant race'.

With Chippindall at the helm, the expeditions were directed from an office at 34 Holborn Viaduct, off Hatton Garden, with the eastern headquarters in Singapore.

The following narrative of a pearling and prospecting cruise is reproduced from *Pearls and Pearling Life*.

In September 1883, the *Sree Pas-Sair* left Singapore in charge of Mr. Chippindall, with a crew of Malay sailors, a Chinese carpenter, cook and 'boy.' In Sooloo, seven men only were shipped, although sixty were required; but these natives had never served a white man before, and were afraid to leave their country. The vessel then proceeded to the island of

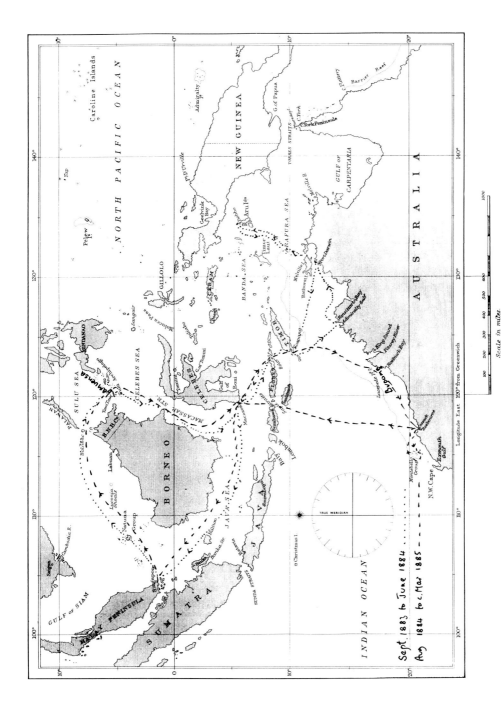

Fig. 89. Chart of the principal pearling regions showing the voyages of the *Sree Pas-Sair*.

Solor, not far from Timor, and having recruited sixty-one Solorese divers, and signed them on before the Dutch Governor at Koepang, Mr. Chippindall sailed for the Australian coast, being accompanied by the late Mr. Harry E. Streeter, a son of the author. There was thus a total of seventy-eight men on board. Admiralty Gulf was visited, and thoroughly searched, but to no purpose; and the vessel continued her course eastwards along the coast, prospecting all the way. At one place seven days were employed in collecting and curing the Chinese dainty, 'beche-de-mer' (Holothuria), this creature being discovered there in profusion. No natives were seen for the first two days, and drying sheds were erected on the beach. Suddenly, however, a body of natives appeared on the scene, and attacked the party in the open. The Solorese jumped into the sea, and swam off to the ship, leaving the white men and the dinghy on the shore. As the spears were flying thickly, and sticking quivering in the sides of the dinghy, the white men were forced to fire for their own protection. The natives soon made off, fortunately without loss of life on either side. Twice again that week attacks were made, and then to avoid bloodshed, the ship left. The remains of a Malay prau were seen here, the crew having been probably murdered by the natives.

The pearling vessel proceeded eastwards, prospecting all the unsurveyed coast up to Port Darwin, but found nothing until that port was reached. On the first day at Port Darwin, 'shell' was struck close to the town, to the great excitement of all the inhabitants, the good news being telegraphed all over Australia. As soon as shell began to get scarce in the shallow water, Mr. Chippindall decided to prospect outside; but the easterly monsoon setting in, he stretched across to the Aru Islands, on his way to New Guinea. Seven days were spent at Dobbo in Aru, and here a strange incident happened, worth mentioning. On attempting to heave up the anchor, it was found to be foul; on sending a man down to report (in $12\frac{1}{2}$ fathoms), it was discovered that the anchor had dropped into a small hole in a rock, standing solitary on a smooth bottom, and that the flukes were firmly fixed below the overhanging edges. The following device was resorted to in order to clear the anchor: a man having gone down, and made fast a small line to the fluke of the anchor in the hole, all chain was veered out to ensure the safety of the ship; four candles of dynamite were bound together with a fuse inserted, and attached to a thimble on the line. The line was then held quite taut and vertical, the fuse lit and the charge dropped, the line being held until the charge was felt to have reached the bottom. The dinghy then paddled away from the spot and the charge was exploded. The result was that the anchor came up with a broken fluke, and the rock was shattered to pieces.

On April 4th, when the New Guinea coast was sighted, a Solorese diver was suddenly taken ill. His pulse being very weak indeed, it was thought that a spoonful of brandy might revive him, but on its being given, the man died in less than a minute.

At New Guinea some chiefs came on board, and were entertained by the mate, whilst Mr. Chippindall pulled ashore some five miles off. Here his dinghy was surrounded by hundreds of canoes with armed savages, but everything passed off well, probably owing to the fact that their own chiefs were on board, and might be looked upon as hostages.

On April 10th another diver died. On the following day very rich ground was found, and some enormous shells were raised. On April 12th the third man died, and Mr. Chippindall, judging from previous experience that more deaths would occur, determined to immediately send the men back to their homes. He therefore sailed that day. By the end of a fortnight the total number of deaths amounted to nine, and while in Port Darwin harbour, in four days, five more died. Every effort was made to rouse the men and distract their attention, but it was useless; the ship was like a charnel house. Meanwhile the seven Sooloo men were looking on, and ridiculing the Solorese as cowards.

During the vessel's absence from Port Darwin, large numbers of boats had arrived from the Torres Straits with diving dresses, and the harbour presented a most lively appearance. They did very well for a short time, but the South-Australian Government, besides enforcing heavy licence fees, offered no inducement to get the coast prospected, and at the present time there is not a single pearling boat left in the waters of the northern territory. The dream of wealth has vanished, and the golden goose is asleep, if not dead.

The fifteenth death occured on May 6th, on arrival at Koepang, where the Solor men were paid off. The last death happened very suddenly in the street, two hours after paying off. The loss in one month was thus sixteen out of the sixty-one men originally shipped from Solor.

The disease from which these men died is called Beri-beri, and it appears to be allied closely to dropsy; large numbers of sailors die of it yearly, and in the tin-mining districts of Perak, there are sometimes as many as 950 Chinamen in hospital at one time. Even the best qualified doctors are at a loss to determine its cause or its cure. Our own experience tends to point to the long-continued rice-diet as the cause, and the natives themselves are beginning to believe this.

In the *Sree Pas-Sair*, the Solorese attributed the deaths to the coast of New Guinea 'being unlucky', but the ship herself remains as popular as ever. The *Flowerdale*, another pearling schooner, has, however, not escaped so well. She lost 19 out of 72 Solorese during the same season, and the men assert that she has a ghost on board, in the form of an old sailor, with a white beard and a long knife. This ghost was supposed to live in the hold in the day and go up aloft at night; and so great was the fear produced, that men would only enter the hold during the day in company with seven or eight others, all joining hands. On suddenly waking at night, the men would declare they saw the ghost touching them with his knife; and screaming with terror, they would fall ill and die in a few hours. The survivors were all in Koepang when the *Sree Pas-Sair* returned; they had refused to put a foot on board the haunted ship again, even for the few hours' run across to their own homes, and the *Sree Pas-Sair* therefore gave them all a passage, eventually arriving in Singapore on the 20th June, and dropping anchor for the 152nd time since she left in the previous September.

On 1st of August, we again find the vessel fitted out for a two years' voyage, and leaving in the charge of Mr. Haynes, bound for the Sooloo Archipelago.

On the way up a dangerous shoal, with only $3\frac{1}{2}$ fathoms of water, was found, in the Koti Passage of the Natuna group. This shoal has been inserted in the latest Admiralty charts, under the name of 'Haynes' Shoal'. Another, but less important reef, was discovered the same week, to the southward of the North Luconia Shoals.

At Sooloo, the seven Sooloo men were gladly welcomed by their friends as returning heroes; and after relating all the experiences of the late voyage, crowds of divers came forward eager to join. Fifty-three men were engaged, including three of the old hands, and the ship sailed for Macassar and Australia.

It was interesting to observe the demeanour of these new men. They were proceeding to unknown lands, under the control of a white man, for the first time in their lives; the ship was equally strange to them, and a superstitious feeling of approaching awe was aroused. In the Straits of Macassar, at night, the ship passed slowly close to a great mass of floating wood, probably some tree brought down by a river in Borneo. This tree had been taken possession of by sea-birds for a roosting-place, and being suddenly alarmed by the close approach of the ship, the birds took flight, flapping their wings, and running along the surface of the water, making considerable noise before they were fairly on the wing. The sleeping Sooloo men were aroused just in time to distinguish the black mass on the water, fading away into the darkness astern. This phenomenon effectually disposed of further sleep that night. In the morning several of the elder men came to their master, and gravely, and with timidity, enquired whether 'that were Satan they saw last night!' In Macassar, Mr. Chippindall again joined the ship, and took charge; he and Mr. Haynes proceeding to Australia, and the mate leaving the ship.

Cossack, the headquarters of the West Australian pearling fleet, was reached in due time. Here a new mate joined, and work was begun at the head of the Exmouth Gulf. From April to October it is fine, calm, clear water, but too cold for naked diving. Even in November the water in the Gulf was standing at 68 degrees Fahr., and the atmosphere at 72 degrees Fahr., while all the boats were necessarily idle. Such cold would be sufficient to kill men if they dived.

There was one other schooner with Solorese on board, but all the others were working West-Australian aborigines. These men dive feet first, and turn in the water; such a method being far less exhausting than plunging head foremost. The Solorese imitated the Australian men, but the Sooloo men would not give up their old habits, and they treated the latter with the utmost contempt as unclean animals. The Australians, however, proved themselves by far the best shell-getters.

In order to avoid the excessive cold, the *Sree Pas-Sair* and another boat went north, to the Montebello group[1] where the water was quite warm and clear. This was the first time the group had ever been dived, and magnificent shells were found averaging 380 pairs to the ton. (The West Australian technical term is 'a pair of shells,' i.e. one oyster). Six weeks of steady diving went on, and after 'their ears were broken,' the Sooloo men did fairly well. If a man ceases to dive for a few months, he experiences great pain in his ears on again commencing, and this is slightly alleviated by oil and laudanum. After persevering from four to six days, something suddenly appears to give way in the ears when under water, and then all pain disappears; the man can at once proceed to greater depths, and will suffer no inconvenience for the rest of the season. There is no discharge of blood, neither is the sense of hearing impaired.

Christmas day was spent at the Montebellos; and on Boxing day a magnificent Pearl weighing 40 grains was found. This is the finest and best-shaped Pearl yet obtained from this coast. As the fresh water was now running short, a likely spot was decided upon, and a well was sunk through 20 feet of rock, below which a fair supply of good water was fortunately found. A beacon has now been erected to guide vessels into the group and to the well of fresh water.

Early in January the two ships returned to the Gulf, finding the water warm at last, and all the other pearlers doing fairly well, but the ground did not suit the Sooloo men.

In February all the fleet went into a creek and beached for shelter, the barometer having fallen unusually low, and the weather looking very threatening, but they escaped without a 'blow' and returned to work after four days. As stinging weed and fishes were plentiful, and the water was very thick, the *Sree Pas-Sair* and the *Ivy* returned to the Montebellos. Beautiful weather set in, and every morning the water was as smooth as oil, the shell being seen from the top. The daily work was performed with ease and profit; but unfortunately 'Beri-beri' commenced to show itself amongst the Sooloo men. A dropsical tendency appeared, and half the men had to stop work. A house was built ashore, and flour substituted for rice,

---

1 Haynes was to return to Montebello in 1909 when he founded the Montebello Shell Syndicate Ltd. to produce cultured shell. The company did not prosper and was wound up in 1917. Captain J.R. Gray, with Ernestine Hill on the yacht *Silver Gull*, visited the site in 1935, when they did have success in cultivating shell. The Islands became the site for British atom bomb tests in 1952.

and to this is attributed the unusually low mortality. Four men died, and to save the others, a premature return had to be made. Cossack was again visited, to obtain the ship's papers, and to pay the duty of £4 per ton on the shells obtained.

A course was then laid for Macassar, and a fair run made to Sapie Straits, but three more poor fellows died on the way across, two of them within twelve hours of their first complaining of illness. This brought the total number of deaths up to seven, and happily then all sickness disappeared. Strange to say, these Sooloo men showed great apathy at the loss of their comrades; they made no noisy lamentations over them, and as soon as a body was committed to the deep, the occurrence was apparently forgotten. Had there been a panic amongst them, the deaths would probably have been trebled, as many of the men showed symptoms of the disease. Fortunately, there was a deck-load of cows and sheep, which kept the men employed and interested. The boxing gloves were also got up, and the men were instructed in the art of self-defence, in order to distract their attention, great merriment being caused by many of the combats.

At the entrance to the Sapie Straits the ship was becalmed for six days, and the men had very hard work towing the ship all day. Every afternoon a little wind sprang up, and the unfathomable straits were entered; but after a couple of miles the wind died away, and the ship being caught by the furious ebb tide, was sent helpless out to sea again, the tide rips and whirlpools spinning her round and round. On the sixth day the last tank of fresh water was broached, and the unsurveyed Western passage was that night attempted and successfully made. Water and grass were obtained from one of the islands, and Macassar was soon reached.

Here the Sooloo men were paid their wages, so that they might invest in goods, thereby greatly increasing their earnings by selling their purchases in their own country. It spoke well for their acquired habits of confidence and discipline, that they accepted their master's statement as to the amount due to each, with silent approval and without question.

A rule had been made that no wages should be paid for days lost by sickness, in order to deter the lazier men from feigning illness; and the justice of this rule is highly appreciated by the industrious men themselves. It is often difficult to determine whether a complaining man is, or is not, skulking, but it is much safer, if in doubt, to permit him to remain on board though well, than to order him out to dive, even at the risk of creating discontent among the more honest and industrious of the ship's company.

Two days' liberty were given to the men, who quickly exchanged their wages for goods. An English acrobatic company happened to be in Macassar at the time, and all the hands were taken to see the performance, to the intense delight of all, but especially of the younger men.

Unfortunately the possession of so much money and the excitement of being in a large town proved too much for the mind of one of the divers, Akalal by name, who had hitherto been a slave in his own country, but was now a free man for life, with all a free man's privileges. Impressed with the idea that everybody wanted to rob him of his riches, he became greatly excited; at night he swam off to the ship, clambered up the side, and knocking down the Malay sailor at the cabin door with a belaying pin, he entered the vacant cabin, and there seizing two large krises, attacked his comrades asleep on deck. Fortunately he was secured before doing much harm, and soon became quieter.

Two days afterwards, Mr. Haynes left Macassar in charge of the ship, bound to Sooloo and back again, Mr. Chippindall returning to Singapore. The second day Akalal again broke out, and seriously injured an unoffending Macassar sailor. Mr. Haynes then put him in irons for the remainder of the voyage, and he was kept securely tied up in one of the boats. Indeed, there was considerable difficulty in preserving his life from his comrades, who begged to be allowed to kill him. He gradually became better, but appeared depressed, fearing his probable fate might be to be killed as soon as he left the ship. On the tenth day he was allowed out for two hours for exercise, and then again ironed, but his comrades must have failed to tie him up securely, for that night, the ship being becalmed, and everybody asleep, he managed to get out of the boat, and, ironed as he was, picked up a 9 lb. hand lead, and struck Mr. Haynes on the forehead whilst asleep in a chair on deck, leaving him senseless, covered with blood, and apparently dead, in which state he remained for six hours. The madman then attacked a Sooloo boy, also asleep, but was secured before doing much further harm.

The mate then took charge, and the ship was headed for Macassar, where she arrived four days later. Here Mr. Haynes was most hospitably cared

OPENING OYSTER-SHELLS, COLLECTED BY THE PEARLING FLEET, AND SEARCHING FOR THE PEARLS, ON BOARD MR. STREETER'S SCHOONER, THE "SREE PAS-SAIR."

Fig. 90.

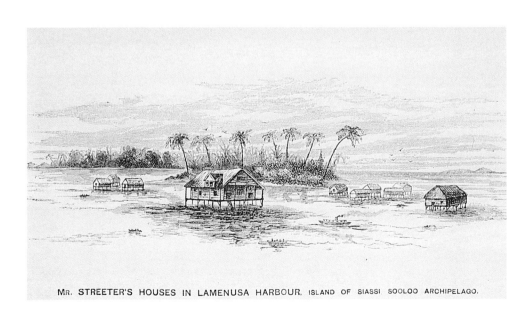

MR. STREETER'S HOUSES IN LAMENUSA HARBOUR, ISLAND OF SIASSI SOOLOO ARCHIPELAGO.

Fig. 91.

for, and kindly tended by a Dutch gentleman for six weeks, and gradually becoming stronger, he recovered his senses of taste and sight, which were temporarily lost. The outer table of the frontal bone was severely fractured, evidence of which will remain visible throughout life; he experiences now but little inconvenience from the injury, beyond that resulting from a permanent loss of the sense of smell.

The Sooloo divers were sent home via Singapore, where the madman was sent to prison, but before leaving Macassar the head-men visited Mr. Haynes to bid him farewell, and actually shed tears to think that one of their number had committed such an outrage.

The late Mr. Chippindall eventually rejoined the ship, and introduced several diving dresses for use on the Australian coast during the cold winter months. It is not difficult to teach natives to become proficient in this work: indeed, several of the Sooloo men were successfully and quickly taught. At the first descent they are, like many white men, very nervous; but if no hitch occurs, they soon regain confidence, and all goes well.

Neither is it difficult, with perseverance, to acquire the art of naked diving. A bright little half-caste boy joined the ship, as apprentice, in Singapore, and at that time he could only get down three fathoms - and even that caused his nose to bleed, - yet he persevered steadily, although he was not expected or even asked to dive, and after five months' practice, could accomplish his ten-and-a-half fathoms. He can now find shells as well as any native.

Mr. Chippindall practically proved that diving dresses could be worked satisfactorily on the North-west Australian grounds, and in a systematic manner. This fact being assured, the use of swimming divers will hence-forth gradually but surely die out. The *Telephone* and the *Sree Pas-Sair* are now used as floating and moveable stations, for the needs of the fleet. Each vessel carries a diving dress and seven men; thus the fleet now consists of 21 boats carrying 150 divers and 21 diving dresses. All these men are signed under shipping articles, and are therefore under complete control. The extended nature of the West Australian pearling grounds, renders this system absolutely necessary, and this will in the future tend to prevent the relations between the masters and the men falling into the state which now exists in Torres Straits.

It speaks well for the discipline of the crew, and the kindness of the officers, that they never have to punish a man, beyond sending him up aloft. Every other night, half of the men come on to the mother ship, to hear the music. The severest punishment the men can receive is not to be allowed to be present at the concert. They work hard and willingly, and being paid so much per pair of shells, no pressing is required to get them to work. By feeding them with flour, mutton, and other food, instead of rice, it is hoped that the dreaded 'Beri-beri' disease may be entirely prevented. The Dutch have just appointed a commission of medical men to enquire into the nature of this dreadful disease, and if possible to devise a remedy.

T. H. Haynes, who provided the information for this narrative, was Streeter's agent in the Sulu Islands and Western Australia. The story goes that the Royal College of Surgeons applied for details and particulars of treatment following the attack on his head with the 9 lb. hand lead. Haynes replied that he attributed his recovery to the fact that no member of the faculty had been able to get to him for ten days. Haynes was to survive this and many other adventures to retire quietly to Littlehampton, Sussex.[1]

The Sulu Archipelago consists of some 150 islands on the north side of Borneo. They are part of the Philippines and in the 1880s, as indeed today, piracy was rife. In *Pearls and Pearling Life* the Sulus are described as 'a strange mixture of villainy and nobility', and the Sulu name is regarded in other islands 'as the synonym of cruelty, treachery and ferocity.'

Haynes came to Lamenusa in February 1883, as Streeter's representative, at the request of the Sultan of Sulu, to lead an exploring party. A Headquarters were erected in the harbour and in February 1884 the Sultan died. His younger brother was elected successor with his mother as Regent. This succession was challenged by the new sultan's uncle, Datoh Aliuddin, and civil war broke out. In March Haynes had to return to Singapore and in his absence Datoh Dakola and Natieb Potch, the adherents of Aliuddin, descended upon Lamenusa in a fleet of war-canoes and destroyed the town of Lamenusa including the pearling station; two unfortunate Chinamen, who were induced by the marauders to place their goods in the station for safety, were also robbed of everything. The Islands were under Spanish sovereignty, the Sultan receiving a pension of $2,400 as recognition of this, so Haynes submitted a claim for compensation to the Sultan, via the Spanish Government, for one house, $1,000 and $500 for goods belonging to the man in charge. A long correspondence ensued, the Lords Rosebery and Salisbury of the Foreign Office being involved. It was

1 *Cossack Gold.* W. Lambden Oliver, Sydney 1933.

stressed that the Spanish Government, by paying a pension to the Sultan, was in a position to enforce the claim which, in the interests of British commerce, should be enforced. However, there was much prevarication by the Spanish authorities and the claim was never settled.[1]

In the early 1880s Haynes established Streeter's business on the Western Australian mainland. At first the headquarters were at Cossack. The earliest activity at Broome was in 1883 when a passage was cleared through the mangroves and a rough jetty erected.[2]

There is evidence that forced slavery of aborigines or 'blackbirding' was used in the expeditions. Harry Streeter reported thus in one of his letters home.

> I wouldn't go pearling with Queensland niggers on any consideration. You have got to ride for a couple of months up country to catch your men, and after you have got them they must be watched night and day to prevent them 'putting'. Then every one on board literally pigs it out during the time they are on the grounds, having to sleep and eat on deck, no matter what weather. Fancy fifty niggers, six white men and 50,000,000 cockroaches all chumming together, and all living on damper and tea.

Harry's letter was printed in the *Pall Mall Gazette* of 5 December 1885 and in the same article there is an interesting account of an expedition by George Streeter, Edwin's second son.

Pall Mall Gazette

Fig. 92. The Fleet at Work

---

1 Public Records Office, F.O. 71/18 and C.O. 144/62 (12182). The author, in 1987, wrote to the Foreign Office asking them to take up the claim again but received no response.

2 Bain, p.227.

The Carpentarian Mother Cooks her Baby

In one of Mr. Streeter's rooms[1] hang a dozen imposing rolls, each of them worked by a string. Pulling the one marked Australia and South Pacific, the whole of that immense area was placed before my eyes by his son. Upon these trackless oceans, studded with a million isles, many of them laid down upon the chart without much pretence to accuracy, for the reefs and the sounds and the channels are always shifting - among these tropical wastes Mr. Streeter's brave little fleet has found its way, and the King of Pearls, although he has never visited foreign parts, is able to follow the various routes which they have adopted, and these are marked by tortuous lines on the map. Somerset, I was informed, was played out. Somerset lies to the north of Carpentaria, and sure enough there was the mark on the map. 'There' said young Mr. Streeter, pointing to Cape York, 'I have done some exploration myself in a modest way. During my visit to the Pacific I fell in with two surveyors who had been commissioned by the South Australian Government to do some land prospecting about the Gulf of Carpentaria. They said they would show me a little life if I would join them, and, nothing loth, we hired a ten-tonner and coasted down the Cape York arm of the great forks which enclose the gulf. We voyaged up many of the of the small rivers which we passed on our way, and had some very hard times. The people are cannibals, and I saw them with my own eyes cook a baby for the table. The Carpentarian mothers have a way of cooking babies, and if they ever miss them, adopt a pigling in their place. The chiefs are fine looking fellows, though I cannot say so much for the women; perhaps the chiefs see this of themselves, for one night we sent up some rockets which frightened them horribly, and the next morning they sent a propitiatory present of forty chosen ladies, whom we returned with thanks. When babies are scarce, they put up with kangaroo flesh, and slugs which they get from the trees. We did not go ashore much, for it was very dangerous, and the waters abounded with alligators.

Around 1885 we find Haynes hiring Japanese divers[2] and an interpreter from Yokohama. The firm exhibited at the Colonial Exhibition in 1886. At this exhibition the Western Australian Court was decorated with columns of mother of pearl shells. The Southern Cross was one of the exhibits. In 1886 two deaths struck the enterprise. Harry died of malaria on his 26th birthday and is

---

1 At 34 Holborn Viaduct, the London headquarters of the pearling ventures.

2 Bain, p.92. The date quoted is wrong.

buried in Fremantle. Captain Chippindall died at Carnot Bay. There were rumours that he had been poisoned by the Malay boatswain of the *Sree Pas-Sair* by putting powdered bamboo into his porridge.[1] George Streeter wrote in his diary when he visited Broome in 1888:

Sept 10th. Arrived at Cossack 10.00am. Called on Robb at the Union Bank and went through the pearling account. Attended the court before Col. Angelo to hear the enquiry on Kerr's death. The man was committed to trial on a charge of wilful murder. Currently stated by men in the court that the same man, who for some time was a sarang on board the *Sree Pas-Sair*, poisoned Chippindall.[2]

By 1890 Broome had superseded Cossack as the main pearling town. In that year the firm built their large store, packing shed and jetty. They erected and subleased the Roebuck Hotel with a view to recouping over the bar the funds paid out to pearlers.[3] They were operating eight schooners and 25 luggers and were employing 500 men.[4] A lease was taken on the 717,000 acre Roebuck Plains sheep station which supplied a butcher's shop.

The farming enterprises were so popular that a milk run was set up.[5] Arthur and Archie Male were employed in the business. They had been born in Dorset and migrated with their parents to Busselton where they worked in the gold fields. Around the turn of the century they became partners and the firm became Streeter and Male.[6]

The 1890s and 1900s were the golden age for pearling at Broome. The pearling masters lived in stylish luxury, sitting on the verandas of their bungalows, diamond studded cufflinks on their shirts, sipping champagne and watching their luggers fishing out at sea. The town gave itself up to the good things of life with the authorities turning a blind eye to the gaming and drinking houses. It should be remembered, however, that mother of pearl was the

---

1 *The Pearl Seekers*. N. Bartlett.

2 The author is in possession of this diary.

3 *Port of Pearls*. H. Edwards, p.4.

4 *Mining Journal*. 23 March 1889.

5 Bain, p.228.

6 *Ibid.*

mainstay of the industry. The income from pearls was an added bonus. Mother of pearl was used for buttons, studs, knife handles, card-cases and ornamental earrings.

By the early part of the new century Broome was producing 80 per cent of the world's mother of pearl. George Streeter spent most of the 1890s in Broome supervising the activities. In 1894 he was nominated by the pearlers to stand in their interests against Alex Forrest, in the elections of that year for the Western Australian Legislative Council.[1] He was defeated by 53 to 28 votes but it was said that if the Torres Islanders and the English had had a vote, the result would have been reversed.[2] George returned to England around 1898. The firm was incorporated as a limited company in 1911 and the Streeter interest sold out to the Males. The decline of the industry started with the disruption of the First World War. In the twenties and thirties the advent of the plastic button and the overfishing of the beds added to the decline.

In 1919 the firm was involved in an attempt to corner the pearl and pearl shell market[3] and control sales in the way that De Beers controlled the sale of diamonds. A company, the Commonwealth Pearl Fisheries Co. Ltd., was formed with two other pearling firms. The authorities got wind of the scheme and it was dropped.

In the 1950s the firm cooperated with the Japanese in setting up a cultured pearl industry in Broome. Today it prospers and is run by Kim Male, Arthur's grandson. The only interest kept up by the Streeter family was the Roebuck Plains Cattle Station. This was finally auctioned in Perth in July 1951.

---

[1] Alexander Forrest (1849-1901) was the younger brother of John Forrest, the first premier of Western Australia. He led a number of exploring expeditions in Western Australia and was later appointed Surveyor General.

[2] Bain, p.229.

[3] Bain, p.293.

Fig. 93.

Fig. 94.

Streeter & Male, Broome. Today.

117

CHAPTER FIVE

THE RUBY MINES OF BURMA

In 1884 Streeter was at a high point in his career. At 50 years of age he had established a flourishing business in Bond Street and was a household name.
He had published two successful books, *Precious Stones and Gems* and *Great Diamonds of the World,* and he was at the forefront in establishing the pearling industry in Western Australia. Amazingly he announced his retirement. An advertisement in the *Illustrated London News* on 4 October 1894 read:

RETIRING FROM BUSINESS.

MR. STREETER,
         18, NEW BOND-STREET,

HAVING, AFTER 38 YEARS' TRADING,

DECIDED TO RETIRE FROM THE

JEWELLERY TRADE,

NOW OFFERS THE WHOLE OF

HIS VALUABLE STOCK OF
      DIAMOND ORNAMENTS,
    18-CARAT GOLD WORK,
    ENGLISH KEYLESS LEVER WATCHES,
    RARE JAPANESE ART WORK,
    AT A GREAT REDUCTION.

THE PUBLIC will for the next few months have special opportunities of securing some of this well-known and carefully selected stock.

MR. STREETER'S COLLECTION of PRECIOUS STONES and GEMS, Rough and Cut, will also be OFFERED for SALE. Connoisseurs and Collectors are invited to inspect.

MR. STREETER, RETIRING FROM BUSINESS,

18, NEW BOND-STREET, LONDON, W.

A sale was duly held at Foster's Sale Room, Pall Mall, starting on 9 December. The preface to the catalogue stated:[1]

---

1 V. & A. Library.

THE FIRST AND SECOND DAY'S SALES offer to Collectors and Connoisseurs in precious stones a most unusual opportunity of acquiring rare gems, as the collection comprises remarkably fine specimens of nearly every known variety, and although Mr. Streeter has enjoyed most exceptional facilities in forming this collection, he having resident agents in all the principal gem-producing districts of the world, it has taken upwards of twenty years to bring it to its present state of perfection. The Curator of one of our principal Scientific and Geological Museums pronounces this collection to be one of the best in existence.

Especial attention may be drawn to the fine Diamonds in matrices: Various forms of crystals, and colours of diamonds, including a set of magnificent large Stars composed of Several Hundred Diamonds of nearly every known tint. Matchless specimens of old Indian, old Brazilian and Cape diamonds, specimen true colour Rubies, and other Rubies from Burma, Ceylon and Siam. A Test Bracelet of perfect stones used by Mr. Streeter for many years. Magnificent suites of colours and shades in Sapphires, including superb cabochon Sapphires of very large size and beauty, and an immense carved Sapphire Cameo. Charming suites of star stones of very great beauty and variety of colours. A number of fine Emeralds in all known matrices, and styles of cutting, including some very fine specimen stones. Remarkable suites of Spinels of great variety of colours. A small collection of unusually fine Pearls and Pearlbearing Shells. Superb suite of Zircons of every colour. Exceptionally fine Tourmalines of great beauty and diversity of hues. Fine specimen Chrysoberyls, Cat's-eyes and Alexandrites, including two rare Alexandrite Cat's-Eyes. Unusually fine Topazes and Peridots. Matchless Opals. Extensive suites of the Garnet family, including the green varieties: also the rare Hiddenite, and many other fancy stones.

THE THIRD DAY'S SALE is composed of Manufactured Stock, the whole of which is mounted in standard 18-carat gold, and the gems, without exception, are set transparent and guaranteed uncoloured; it includes several very beautiful Brilliant Bracelets, a matchless Emerald Suite, a magnificent Opal Suite, fine Pearl and Diamond Earrings, costly Brooches, Pearl Pins and Studs, a number of choice Finger Rings, etc. etc.

The whole sale realized £9,646/15/3d. although not all items matched up to expectations. The catalogue described one lot, No. 92: 'A set of five LARGE STARS, composed of specimens of every known COLOURED DIAMOND, the points of which are composed of black diamonds. It is alleged that the collection of stones comprised in this lot cost over Seven Hundred Pounds.' The lot was sold to a Mr. Trepp for 215 guineas.

However Streeter quickly changed his mind on the question of retirement. He was to enjoy another twenty years of running his shop, financing expeditions and writing books. Culme suggests that he merely took in partners to free capital for expeditions and mining enterprises. This theory is reinforced because the firm in future is designated Streeter & Co. However, there is no other evidence of outside interests and when the business became a limited company in 1895, there were only two shareholders other than Edwin and his immediate family, and they held just 0.4 per cent of the stock. Culme's theory does not explain the announcement to retire and the sale, which remain a mystery.

There is evidence that the business was under different proprietorship for at least a short period because the Post Office Directory for 1886 lists the business as 'Streeter & Co. (Arthur Pitson).' This only occurs for one year. Perhaps Pitson bought the firm for a while and then Streeter bought it back. One piece of jewellery has been traced with 'Arthur Pitson (from Streeter & Co.), 179 New Bond Street' in the box lid. Pitson traded from this address on his own from 1893 until 1922. However, he is not mentioned in Culme's *Directory of Silversmiths* which would indicate that he never had a mark registered with the Goldsmiths' Company.

Fresh capital was certainly found and it was to be expended six thousand miles away in the steaming jungles of Burma. Upper Burma was annexed by the British on 1 January 1886. Lord Randolph Churchill, the Under Secretary, had chosen this date so that the proclamation could be a present to Queen Victoria. On 29 November, the previous year, Mandalay had fallen to General Prendergast and King Thibaw was sent into exile. The pretext for this military adventure was that the Hlutdaw, the Burmese Royal Council, had accused the Bombay-Burma Trading Corporation of fraudulently exporting teak.[1] The real reason for the annexation may have been that the British feared French intervention in the kingdom. Details of the French activity were leaked to the British by the jilted mistress of one of the French community in Mandalay.[2]

Europeans had often wondered about the mysterious ruby mines of Upper Burma, but up to that date the only European visitors were recorded as a runaway English sailor in the employ of King Phagyidoa, who in 1830 was sent

---

1 *The Pagoda War.* A.T.Q. Stewart,. London, 1972.

2 An account of this matter is given by F. Tennyson Jesse in *The Story of Burma*, London, 1946. She also wrote a fictional account, *The Lacquer Lady*, currently in print in Virago Modern Classics.

up to blast a particular rock, and a party of Frenchmen who made the trip in 1881.

One morning in December 1885, Edwin Streeter was breakfasting in the saloon of the Grand Hotel, Paris. He overheard two gentlemen at the same table talking about the Ruby Mines. They mentioned a draft lease from King Thibaw. Edwin's natural interest in the subject led him to join in the conversation and subsequently he was to be introduced to Messrs. Bouveillein & Co., who had obtained the provisional leases for three lakhs.[1] This concession had been granted by the Burmese Ambassador in Paris and it was transferred to Edwin. However, when the British annexed the country, the concession became of no value and the papers were returned.[2]

On returning to England, Streeter wrote to the India Office, who were now in control of Burma, with a view to obtaining the concession. Lord Harris replied that an approach should be made to the Government of India. With two associates, Col. Charles Bill, M.P., and Reginald Beech,[3] Edwin formed a syndicate and engaged the services of Capt. Aubrey Patton as agent,[4] who was dispatched to Calcutta with a letter of introduction to the Viceroy. On arriving at Rangoon, Patton found that Messrs. Gillanders, Arbuthnot had already offered two lakhs (about £14,000) for a lease. The Government was inclined to accept this offer but Patton offered three lakhs. Lord Dufferin decided to exercise caution and put the lease out to tender. The Streeter syndicate's tender was four lakhs and was accepted and draft contracts prepared.

The authorities wished to enquire into the status of any native rights at the mine, and to secure them militarily, so a military expedition was dispatched and George Streeter, Edwin's second son, Charles Bill and Reginald Beech were asked to accompany it. They went up the Irrawaddy to the river port of Thabeitkyin and then through sixty miles of jungle, rampant with malaria and infested with dacoits. They reached Mogok, which is nearly six thousand feet above sea level, on 27 December 1886. The syndicate employed Robert

---

1 A lakh is a hundred thousand rupees (about £7,000).

2 *Precious Stones and Gems.* 6th edition, p.170.

3 Charles Bill (1843-1915). Col. 4th Bn. N. Stafford Militia. Barrister, Lincoln's Inn 1868. M.P. Stafford, 1892-1906.
Reginald Beech (1862-1915). Son of James Beech of Brandon Hall, Warwick. Capt. 4th Bn. Staffordshire Regiment.

4 Later Major Aubrey L. Patton-Bethune and subsequently a director of the Ruby Mine Company. Described by Lord Randolph Churchill as 'an adventurous speculating person, known to fame for his great proficiency in pigeon shooting.' (Dufferin papers, quoted by Stewart in *The Pagoda War*, p.142).

Gordon, an engineer previously in government employ, to survey and map the area. A meeting was held with the local headman to establish the native rights. George Streeter was granted an ordinary mining licence and a monopoly to purchase stones, paying the government 30 per cent duty. Captain Jackson, who also accompanied them as engineer, erected some machinery. The expedition studied the native methods of working. One method used was to dig a large hole shored up with bamboo struts. Often the walls would fall in, burying the miner. Such was the superstition of the others that they would not open the working up again and so a rich seam was lost. George returned home, leaving Frank Atlay,[1] son of the Bishop of Hereford and later the Mine companies' Manager, as the syndicate's agent.

At this stage the proceedings became decidedly murky. Edward Moylan was *The Times'* correspondent in Burma. He had already incurred the displeasure of the authorities by sending back highly coloured accounts of the British Army's behaviour during the fall of Mandalay, and General Prendergast had him deported back to Rangoon. Moylan, however, used influence back home and had himself reinstated. Dufferin had enquiries made into Moylan's past. He found that he had been suspended as Attorney-General of Grenada, West Indies, for bringing the administration into disgrace and subsequently disbarred from practising as a barrister on the same island for misconduct. On losing the tender, Gillanders Arbuthnot employed Moylan as their legal adviser. He subsequently filled *The Times* and local papers with accusations about the rival company, including that it contained Frenchmen.

The syndicate contained in fact no Frenchmen but a jeweller of 37 Boulevard Haussmann, Paris, entered the stage in the shape of Mr. Moritz Unger,[2] a German by birth but a British naturalized citizen.

---

1 Henry Francis Atlay (1862-1923) was the second son of the Bishop of Hereford. He was in business in Manchester, then Calcutta, before becoming the agent for the Ruby Company in Burma. In his will he left 500 rupees to his servant Abdool; 250 rupees to his servant Gugbir, 'my gun carrier on many happy days'; his books to the Pegu Club, Rangoon; a pair of elephant tusks to Wellington College (his old school, which he entered in the same term as Reginald Beech); and the income from 15,000 rupees to one Ma Piya Mai. Montague J. Battye, Secretary of the Burma Ruby Mine Co. (1855-94) was also an Old Wellingtonian entering the school three years before Atlay and Beech.

2 Moritz Unger was very active in the South African goldfields at the time of Thomas Tobin's expedition. He traded as a diamond merchant and was prominent in local affairs. His career was interrupted when Leopold Lowenthal, representing creditors of a bankruptcy incurred by Unger in Edinburgh, took him to Court. The case was thrown out on the grounds that Scottish law had no remit in a territory that was not yet even a Colony.

Mr. Unger announced that he was an agent of a wealthy syndicate of European capitalists based in Paris, headed by the Rothschilds, and he added that the concession was worth twelve times the offer actually accepted. Unger was asked for details of his principals but did not produce them. He was disbarred from visiting the mines and numerous reports of Unger's and Gillanders' disappointments filtered back to the British press. Thirty seven questions were asked in Parliament. Thirty four of these were from Charles Bradlaugh,[1] the firebrand Radical from Northampton. Because two members of the Streeter syndicate, together with their engineer, Captain Jackson, had accompanied the military expedition to the mines, he maintained that government officials had been bribed. Also he stated that Gillanders and Unger were being treated unfairly and being prevented from competing. Hugh Watt, the Member for Glasgow Camlachie, accused George Baird, who had, with George Streeter, joined the syndicate, of being of bad character and repute as he had been recently prosecuted. Sir John Gorst, the Under Secretary, replied that Baird had been prosecuted under the Foreign Enlistment Act but been acquitted. The India Office was put out of step by all this publicity so Lord Cross, the Secretary of State, commissioned a geologist, Mr. C. Barrington-Brown, to undertake a full survey of the mines to establish their actual worth.

The lease between the Government and the syndicate was finally signed on 22 February 1889. It is not clear if Mr. Unger ever represented Rothschilds. In his diary for 30 April 1887, George Streeter in Rangoon records:

> The mail boat *Secundra* got under way at daybreak, very crowded, every berth taken. Spent the morning in copying agreement. Rest of the day reading and walking. Found five curious little Japanese women on board going to Calcutta. Had a talk with Mr. Reid of the National Bank who assured me Moritz Unger never represented the Rothschilds, but that a French syndicate applied to his bank for a clear credit of £10,000 which they refused to give without £5,000 that was deposited. They then went to Rothschilds, deposited the money, and got a credit from him.

But by 1889 the firm of N.M. Rothschild and Sons were involved. Two years earlier the Exploration Company, a mining finance house headed by Leopold de Rothschild, and composed of the leading bankers and stockbrokers of the day, had written to the Secretary for India, enquiring if they could bid for the mines. The Exploration Company was powerful in mining finance and the Streeter

---

1 Charles Bradlaugh (1833-91) was M.P. for Northampton from 1880 to 1891 although he was unable to take his seat until 1885 because he insisted on affirming rather than swearing the Oath of Allegiance.

A Glimpse of the Burma Mines.

Purchasers of Rubies who are in any doubt as to their genuineness are invited to send them for examination to—

THE BURMA RUBY MINES LTD.

SUFFOLK HOUSE,
LAURENCE POUNTNEY HILL, LONDON, E.C.

It is advisable when purchasing Rubies to specify BURMA RUBIES and to insist on invoice with definite statement to this effect.

Sorters at Work.

Fig. 95. A page from a leaflet issued by the Burma Ruby Mines Ltd.

syndicate wisely joined with them and Rothschilds to form and float the Burma Ruby Mines Ltd. Without exaggeration it can be said that the issue was one of the most sensational of the century. The prospectus was published on 26 February 1889. There was such a scrummage in New Court of investors seeking application forms, that Lord Rothschild was forced to gain access to his office with the help of a ladder through a back window.[1] The offer was oversubscribed fourteen times and the ordinary shares shot to a 400 per cent premium, while the £1 founders' shares were trading at a staggering £350. Father and son Streeter would have done well, both by the sale of their share of the syndicate to the company, and by the premiums on the shares they were allotted.

Following such a spectacular start, the company was to run into difficulties and the shares languished. Sir Lepel Griffin,[2] the Chairman, presided at a general meeting in June 1889.[3] Firstly he reported on the disturbed state of Upper Burma. The country was ravaged by dacoits but he had every confidence in the administration and was sure that the territory could be pacified. Next he alluded to the sixty-four miles of road that had to be built through jungle from the Irrawaddy to the mines. It was hoped that the road would be finished by January. Sir Lepel went on to say that the road was more important than the dacoits 'because we can shoot the dacoits but without the road we cannot get our machinery to the mines.' The final problem reported upon was smuggling, for which there was a 2,000 year old tradition. Smuggling today is still a problem and for this reason foreigners are not allowed to go to Mogok. The vote of thanks to the board was proposed by Mr. Unger, now a shareholder, who must have felt that as he couldn't beat them, he should join them.

Difficult working conditions continued. The richest ruby-bearing gravel was found under the town of Mogok and the surrounding paddy fields. The whole of this land had to be purchased and the buildings of the town dismantled and re-erected, a long and expensive business.[4] Transporting the heavy pumping

---

1 *The Mining Journal,* London, 2 March 1889.

2 Sir Lepel Griffin retired in January 1889 from a successful career as an Indian Civil Servant. He had been Secretary to the Governor of the Punjab, Chief Political Officer in Afghanistan and Resident in Hyderabad. He was also Chairman of the Imperial Bank of Persia.

3 *Financial News,* London, 26 June 1889.

4 Col. J.F.Halford-Watkins, *The Book of Ruby and Sapphire.* Unpublished manuscript. Library of the Gemmological Association.

plant and machinery was a considerable task. The road, in effect a rough mule track, was finished after a year. It passed through dense jungle infested with wild animals and dacoits, over mountains 5,000 feet high. Bullock carts were the only vehicle and the journey was three weeks in dry weather; in the six months of the wet season, the route was impassable. Rinderpest broke out. The bullocks died wholesale and the machinery was held up for months on end.

All these difficulties were overcome and the Government assisted by writing off some of the back rent and agreeing to a new reduced rent. In 1898/99 the company was able to announce its first dividend of 5 per cent and from then onwards, dividends were the rule rather than the exception.

Firstly the mines were open-cast but later a system of washing down the earth with high pressure jets and passing it through sluice-boxes was instigated. Mainly owing to the endemic smuggling, a monopoly of supply, like that obtained for diamonds in South Africa, was never achieved. The invention of the synthetic ruby in 1908 dented the market but the company continued until 1925, when it went into voluntary liquidation. The lease was finally surrendered to the Government in 1931.

CHAPTER SIX

SAPPHIRES FROM MONTANA

I n 1882 Streeter wrote in *Precious Stones and Gems* that at the present price
level, the importing of Brazilian diamonds was unpropitious. However, he
had in his library, *Pioneering in South Brazil,*[1] by Thomas Bigg-Wither, who
wrote in 1878 that the diamond fields of Tibagi 'are capable, with improved
methods of washing and an intelligent management, of yielding a further large
profit.' An advertisement in December's *Illustrated London News* of 1886
announced that the firm had acquired special rights in the new and productive
diamond fields of Tibagi in Brazil. No more of this particular concession is
heard but Streeter was to be infected with prospecting fever again, with
thoughts of sapphires and rubies in the state of Montana, U.S.A.

The Sapphire and Ruby Company of Montana Ltd. was formed in September
1891 to acquire 8,000 acres of properties in that state. Lord Chelmsford[2] was
Chairman and E. W. Streeter one of the seven directors. As soon as the
prospectus was issued, the financial press fell about themselves with laughter
and amazement. The *Financial Observer and Mining Herald* on

---

1 This volume was included in a list of books donated by Streeter to the Goldsmiths'
Company.

2 By contrast to Sir Lepel Griffin, Chairman of the Burma Ruby Mines Ltd.,
Lord Chelmsford's previous career was marked by some spectacular disasters. He was
Commander-in-Chief in South Africa in 1879 during the Zulu Wars. He had 5,000
European troops and 8,000 armed natives in his command. He decided to operate in three
columns. The right under Col. Pearson crossed the Tegula. The centre, under Chelmsford,
crossed the Buffalo at Rorke's Drift, and the left, under Sir Evelyn Cross, crossed the Blood
River to the North. On 22 January 1880 at Isandula, Chelmsford with a party of troops left
his column to join a scouting party ten miles ahead. At midnight the camp was attacked by
10,000 Zulus. 860 Europeans were killed and three survived. Thus occurred one of the most
devastating massacres in the annals of the British Army. While Chelmsford was
groping in the darkness around the debris of Isandula, another battle was being fought a few
miles away. At Rorke's Drift a small garrison fought off 3,000 Zulus. Eleven V.C.s were
awarded and the action was the subject of the film *Zulu*. A further disaster followed when
the Prince Imperial, Head of the Imperial House of Bonaparte, then living in exile in
England, came out as a non-combatant. Soon after his arrival he went on a scouting party
into an ambush. Part of the troop rode off and he and three others were killed. England was
horrified by these disasters and Chelmsford was replaced by Sir Garnet Wolseley. Before
Wolseley arrived however, Chelmsford regained some stature by defeating the Zulus at
Ulundi. (*The Zulu Kings*, Brian Roberts, and *D.N.B.*).

29 August 1891 started off with a broadside of puns. They observed that the promoters were using green sapphires to entice green shareholders. Then, noticing that the vendor of the mine and one of the promoters was a Mr. Spratt, they suggested that a sprat was being used to catch a mackerel. When the prospectus stated, 'On the lands to be acquired by the Company careful prospecting demonstrated the existence of Sapphires and Rubies - chiefly the former - in quantities unprecedented in the history of gem discovery', the journal went on to comment:

If we can stand that, we can stand anything, and nothing after this within the repertoire of either Baron Munchausen or Sancho Panza, should be too large for our swallow. There is, we take it, very little working necessary, no cumbrous and costly plant and machinery, only sacks to put the stones in, and labour being cheap and probably dishonest, can be employed in picking up rubies (as big as walnuts), sapphires (the size of brazil-nuts) and other less valuable gems (running about the size of cocoa nuts) in the same way, and in somewhat the same style that they do turnips here, only it is easier, the gems lying about in profusion simply waiting to be picked up, a process applying just now more particularly to the proposed sharehold-ers.

On the passage in the prospectus 'assuming an annual sale of the product of only ten acres, the result would be a net return of over £188,000 per annum, equal (after allowing £6,000 for depreciation contingencies etc.) to more than 40 per cent upon the capital of the company', they exclaimed:

Bah! what is 40 per cent to us per annum, why, we have been reckoning that per minute, twice per minute in fact. Of course, this is only on ten acres, and there are 4,000, so multiply £188,000 by 4,000, and it is not perhaps so bad: and if it had been per month, or better still, per week, it would have fitted in with our preconceived ideas a bit, but still it would not have come up to them by a street. 27,104 carats at 20 shillings per carat would yield £27,104, and twenty-seven million carats, of course, so much more. We don't care about seeing the other reports on this very wonderful and extraordinary freak of - company-mongering.

The *Lighthouse* reported, in their issue of 31 October 1891, that they had submitted the flowery prospectus to a mining expert. The opinion they obtained was 'far too emphatic for a law-abiding paper to publish.' The same paper commented that Streeter had been involved with the Burma Ruby Mines Company which had run into its difficulties and the shares fallen.

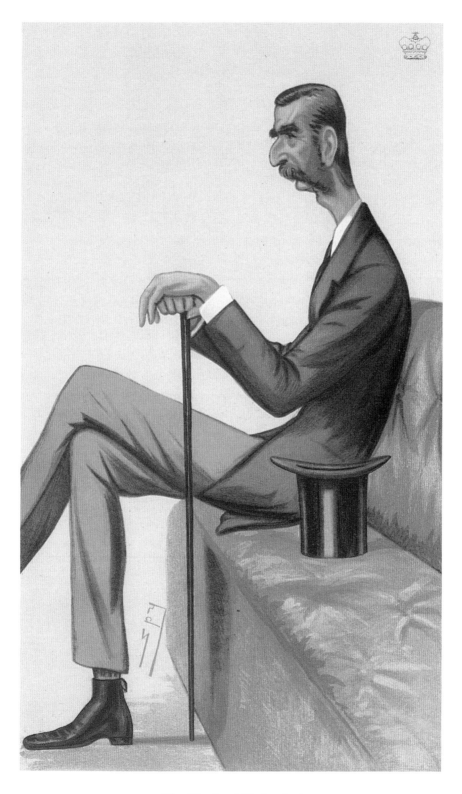

Fig. 96. Lord Chelmsford.

131

The *Financial Observer and Mining Herald* returned to the onslaught on 7 November. They implored investors 'to withdraw their applications at once by wire and registered letter for they are caught in a trap.' They go on to expose the experts who have reported on the mines. They suggest that the samples of stones brought back have been 'salted' so as to deceive. They attack Lord Chelmsford as knowing nothing about gems and remark that he was a failure in the army. Finally, the article highlights one aspect of the prospectus which had all the financial commentators gasping. This was that 'No part of the purchase money will be paid to the vendors until two or more of the directors of the company shall have visited and approved the property.' Why didn't the directors visit the property before issuing the prospectus and are not their findings predictable? A chorus of journalists asked.

In November 1891 Streeter, and fellow director, H. Mallaby-Deeley,[1] set off for the U.S.A. to write their report. In New York they engaged an independent mineralogist, J. D. Yewington, and on the 11 December they cabled back 'Examination of the Sapphire Mines completed. We are perfectly satisfied in every point. The great value of the property cannot be questioned. We approve the purchase.'[2] The full reports written in January were glowing.[3] The company was to be allowed an extra 4,000 acres and therefore a monopoly of the stones in the area. Sapphires weighing 20,000 carats were obtained. There were good markets in the U.S.A. for the stones and to cap it all the terrain was also gold-bearing.

In January of 1892, the *Star*[4] reported that proceedings, on the grounds of misrepresentation, had been started by a shareholder to recover money. The

---

1 Harry Mallaby-Deeley subsequently was to enjoy a prosperous business career. He became celebrated as a 50/- tailor. Then, in 1919, he pulled off a coup by purchasing the inheritance of Lord Edward Fitzgerald, the bankrupt heir to the demented Duke of Leinster. Lord Edward had run up debts of some £60,000 but would not inherit the family fortune until his invalid elder brother, then aged 32, died. Mallaby-Deeley paid off all the debts. The 6th Duke conveniently died three years later and he came into all the ducal property. In the inter-war years he consolidated his fortune with some spectacular property deals involving the Covent Garden Estate, Foundling Hospital Estate and St. George's Hospital. He built up the Princes Golf Club at Sandwich and Mitcham and became Conservative M.P. for Harrow from 1910 to 1918 and Willesden from 1918 to 1923. Created a baronet in 1922, he died in his chateau in Cannes in 1937. (*The Times* obit. 6 February 1937; *The Dukes*, Brian Masters, 1975).

2 The *Star*, 11 December 1891.

3 *Financial News*, 27 August 1872.

4 The *Star*, 23 January 1892.

Fig. 97. Sir Harry Mallaby-Deeley

promoters blandly carried on and in December of that year, there was an exhibition at 18 New Bond Street of a consignment of sapphires from Montana. The *Morning Post* reported:

> The sapphires shown on Saturday were an excellent sample, pure in colour but of varying shades, and those made up in a variety of settings excited universal admiration. Rubies, diamonds, and gold from the same district were also shown, and Mr. Streeter expressed the opinion that Montana is likely to become a formidable rival to the gem-producing countries of the Old World.

By the time of the third Annual General Meeting of the Company, a sense of reality had descended upon the directors. Lord Chelmsford expressed regret at the unsatisfactory nature of the accounts, and he hoped the shareholders would not be antagonistic. A Mr. Judd spoke on behalf of the shareholders' committee. He stated that they were astonished at the culpable stupidity of the Board. He suggested that, as they had not all been paid for, the names on the founders' shares had been inserted as decoys. He compared the proposed income per annum of £188,000 to the actual of £600 and concluded that the company had proved an utter failure.

The full story was to be set out in the report of the investigation committee published in December 1894.[1] The committee found that the list of subscribers to the founders' shares[2] in the prospectus - which included two Dukes, three Marquises, seven Earls, over a dozen Barons and numerous Knights and Baronets - was designed to induce subscribers to invest, particularly as these founder shareholders had guaranteed to underwrite the ordinary shares but most of them had failed to honour their guarantee. The report found that two directors, H. Mallaby-Deeley and Mr. Gurney Littlewood, had not paid calls on their shares and so, under the articles of the company, were not bona fide directors. It went on to reveal that, as the underwriters failed to pay for their shares, the company had difficulty in completing its purchase contract for £200,000 cash and £200,000 in shares. The vendors then rescinded the contract and another one was completed offering more land for £28,268 cash and £371,732 in shares. Legal action by the shareholders against the directors was recommended but this was deferred pending further counsel's opinion. The company was saved from ignominy by being taken over in 1898 by the Eldorado Gold and Gem Co. of Montana Ltd. (incorporated in Michigan). Edwin Streeter survived this fiasco although, as we shall see, he was none the wiser for it. Naivety and ridiculous optimism were his principal sins. He lost money, being a subscriber to one founder share and 250 ordinary shares at the launching and holding 1,530 ordinary shares shortly before the liquidation. His son, George, appears to have been more level-headed over the matter. He visited the mines in March of 1890. His diary entries for this period are brief but there are signs of scepticism.

In December George resigned from the Board of a company called Sapphires and Rubies of Siam Ltd.[3] whose Chairman, Lord Thurlow, was a founder subscriber of the Montana Company. This would indicate apprehension about such schemes and there are signs that George, from this time onwards, distanced himself from his father's more extravagant enterprises.

---

1 *Financial News,* 6 December 1894.

2 The method of allocating shares may have been similar to that used by Sir Thomas Lipton, who gave first precedence to Dukes, then Marquises, and so on down the social order.

3 George Streeter's diaries.

CHAPTER SEVEN

TASKER v. STREETER

In the 1895 Edition of *Kelly's Post Office Directory*, Edwin was listed as:

> Streeter & Co. diamond & gem merchants, pearlers, goldsmiths, jewellers & lapidaries, London, Ceylon, Burma, Siam & Western Australia: precious stones & gems scientifically cut on the premises, 18 New Bond Street W (T. A. 'Safeguard'; T. N. 35298) & 16 Glasshouse Street W. Estab. 1670. Streeter, Mr. F.R.G.S. lapidist, pearler, miner & diamond merchant, precious stones received in rough direct from the principal mines of the world, 18 New Bond St. W.

In the same year he moved to 2 Park Crescent, the impressive Nash terrace to the south of Regent's Park. The claim in the notice that the firm was established in 1670 has no foundation. There was a Walter Streeter apprenticed to Thomas Harris, goldsmith, in 1671 but there is no evidence that he had any connection with Edwin. In earlier advertisements it was stated that the firm was established in the reign of George III. This claim, although tenuous, has more substance and refers to the founding of Emanuel's in 1802. Edwin took over the premises and presumably the goodwill of this firm in 1873, but not the stock.

In November 1895 and March 1896 Edwin was the subject of biographical articles in both the monthly magazine *Women at Home* and the *Evening News*. The *Evening News* article has inaccuracies but, in the absence of surviving personal correspondence and contemporary memoirs, these articles do give an impression of our subject's character. He comes over as cheerful, industrious, avuncular and fond of a joke. He certainly was not a workaholic. George Streeter recalls in his diary that one day he called into his father's office to see him only to find that he had gone off to the Windsor Show. The *Evening News* [1] mentions a fondness for reading and an interest in gentleman farming at the country seat in Sussex.[2]

Kelly's Directory for Sussex lists Edwin as amongst the principal landowners in the village of Buxted. In 1882 Thomas Claydon is mentioned as his farm bailiff at 'The Box'. Perhaps it was here that it was proposed to shell the odoriferous oysters. The *Evening News* describes him as being fond of

---

1   21 March 1896.

2   Wrongly given as Derbyshire in the article.

gardening, an authority on carrots and never happier than when out with his pack of beagles. Generosity was also one of his virtues. He would send, unsolicited, precious stones to museums around the world so that the knowledge of them could be more widely spread.

Public spiritedness was another virtue. In April, two disarming individuals called on him at New Bond Street, collecting for the Lord Mayor's Fund for orphans of the Zulu War. Before he could subscribe to their collection, he was called away on business and when he returned they had gone. The ruse had been attempted on other businesses and Edwin went into print[1] to warn the general public, describing the villains as having the appearance of military men, one in a light grey shooting suit, the other, in a navy blue pilot suit, and speaking with a broad Scottish accent and lisp.

On another occasion Lord Calthorpe, worried by the export of breeding mares, sent out an appeal to his fellow aristocrats and landowners for a fund to subsidise stallions so as to maintain a good breeding stock of farming horses. The appeal did not reach its target so Edwin wrote to *The Times,* suggesting: 'There are numbers of tradesmen in London (springing from the country) who are lovers of a good horse, and who would, if appealed to, quickly raise the required sum. I endorse this opinion by hereby offering the sum of £100 towards Lord Calthorpe's Fund, providing 49 other business men will follow suit.'

The *Women at Home* article also mentions instances of robberies from the shop. On the first occasion, a gentleman came in to look at some articles, among which were some five unset diamonds. Whilst looking at these he fixed a portion of cobbler's wax under the ledge of the counter and pressed one of the diamonds in it. Later a lady entered and while she was making some small purchases it was noticed that she slipped something into her pocket. She was apprehended with the cobbler's wax and diamond. On the other occasion, a very attractive young lady entered while Edwin was showing a wealthy customer some important pieces. She came over to the counter and leaning on it with her muff, admired the specimens, but did not purchase. Soon after she left, it was discovered that a diamond and ruby locket valued at £10,000 was missing. The locket was later noticed in a New York jeweller's window but nothing could be done as there was no extradition treaty with the U.S. However, the beautiful thief was caught red handed employing the same technique in Paris. It was discovered that in her muff was a spring pocket that opened upon being pressed and shut when released.

For security all jewellery was packed into strong boxes and mechanically lowered to the basement strongroom. When one assistant was serving, others were trained to keep a watch. There were looking glasses all round the shop

---

1 *The Times,* 9 June 1875.

and further surveillance was provided by the clerks in the counting house who were housed in a balcony around the showroom.

An insight into life in the Victorian West End of London comes from the case of *Tasker v. Streeter and Co.,* heard in the High Court in February and March 1895. Joseph Charles Tasker, at the age of 24, inherited £700,000. The fortune came from a distant cousin, Joseph Tasker, a stockbroker. His heir was his daughter, Helen Ann, who did not marry but so devoted herself to Catholic good causes that the Pope in 1870 created her a Countess. The inheritance was held in trust for the Countess and had to be inherited by a male heir, so when she died in 1888 leaving an estate of £301,251, the settlement came eventually to her distant cousin, Joseph. The *Daily News,* which unearthed the history of the fortune, gives its value at the time of Joseph's inheritance at £500,000 but the figure to be given in court was £700,000.[1]

In May 1894, when Tasker was 25, he was taken by Baron von Orsbach, his former tutor, to see the model of the Gates of the Holy City at 18 New Bond Street. He was introduced to Mr. Streeter; then Mr. Samuel Rogers, the manager and buyer, showed him a pearl which he purchased for £500. Rogers brought the pearl round to Tasker's rooms at the Belgravia Hotel later that day, together with a diamond ring which he also purchased for £300. Rogers saw Tasker the following day and sold him the model of the Holy City for £1,500. He also took an order for a silver model of Tasker's yacht, *Zingara,* which he had bought in Bombay for £7,000 and a photograph of which was on the wall. The cost was £300 and it was to be disputed if this included a silver stand or if the stand was £150 extra. Subsequently, Rogers brought the *Stafford* Collection of gems to his rooms, which Tasker agreed to buy for £10,000, and he gave a cheque for this amount.

Later he bought by cheque a pair of black pearl and diamond earrings with brooch for £5,000. Rogers also discussed with Tasker the purchase of the *Agra* diamond,[2] which he said had cost his firm £14,000, for £15,000 and the purchase of the *Hope* diamond for £32,000.

The *Hope* diamond had belonged to Lord Francis Hope, but he had gone bankrupt and the stone was currently under the control of the Court of Chancery. Streeters were to negotiate its release. Rogers obtained Bills of Exchange from Tasker for £15,000 which he signed in bed. Later he obtained a cheque for £51,625, covering the cost of the *Hope* diamond at £32,000, Bow Brooch at £5,000, *Agra* diamond at £15,000, less discount £375. The cheque was subsequently stopped.

---

1 *Daily News.* 1 March 1895.

2 For a history of the *Agra* diamond, see Appendix 3.

MR. STREETER.

MR. TASKER.

MR. ROGERS.

Fig. 98. Illustrations in the Sunday newspapers of the principal characters in the case of
Tasker v. Streeter.

138

Many of these transactions were in fact conducted while Mr. Tasker was in bed and his counsel alleged that this was because he was either intoxicated with alcohol or recovering from intoxication.

One evening in June, Tasker had returned to bed with gout. Rogers was summoned to dine by telegram and he came accompanied by Rowe, Streeter's secretary, and a Mr. Vickers, a Bond Street picture dealer. Tasker must have recovered from his gout, for the party dined, went out to a theatre and returned to the Belgravia Hotel for another dinner. At two o'clock in the morning, Rogers produced from his pocket, a set of diamonds on approval from Messrs. Alexander of Hatton Garden, saying he had no business to show them to anybody as they were not properly on the market, but he would show them to Tasker out of kindness and he offered them to him for £30,000. Tasker declined the offer and said he would not do business at that time of the morning.

Later in June Tasker suffered remorse over these somewhat extravagant transactions (in a space of three weeks he had spent £100,500 on jewellery, one seventh of his patrimony). He felt, owing to his drunkenness and ignorance of precious stones, advantage had been taken of him. He claimed that for a number of the transactions no contracts existed and that his outstanding Bill of Exchange and cheques should be returned. Rogers and Rowe, Streeter's secretary, sought an out of court settlement but Tasker's solicitor called them a pair of thieves and negotiations broke down.

The case came to court and was heard by Mr. Baron Pollock[1] and a special jury at the Queen's Bench division. The first day's hearing was on Friday, 22 February, Mr. Findlay Q.C. and Mr. Darling Q.C. for Tasker and Sir Edward Clarke Q.C.[2] for the defendants. Sir Edward was particularly qualified to undertake this brief as he had spent four years in his teens assisting his father in the family silversmith and jeweller's shop. From the time he became Q.C. in 1892, he was one of the most eminent leaders of the Common Law Bar.

Mr. Findlay started by summing up his client's case. He said the action was brought so as to set aside, or declare invalid, certain alleged purchases. He admitted that for the period in question, his client was in feeble health owing to intemperate habits. He suggested that during this time Mr. Rogers devoted himself to him - lunching with him, dining with him and constantly in his company. He stated that the items in dispute were the *Agra* diamond, costing £15,000 and a diamond Bow Brooch costing £5,000. The *Agra* had been

---

1 Report of the Tasker case can be found in *The Times, Daily Telegraph, Globe, Standard* and *News of the World* from 23 February to 1 March 1885.

2 Sir Edward Clarke (1841-1931) was the son of Job Guy Clarke, Jeweller and Silversmith of 15 King William Street E.C. Admitted to Bar 1864. Q.C. 1892. M.P. (C) Plymouth 1880-1900. Solicitor General 1886-92.

represented to Tasker as costing £14,000 but, in fact, Streeter's had obtained it from Hertz & Co. of Paris with an exchange of pearls worth £15,000 for the *Agra* and £1,000 cash.

Findlay ended by asking the jury if it was proper that a canvasser such as Mr. Rogers should be put upon a young man like the plaintiff, whose health was such that anyone seeing him would see that he was not fit to transact business, and by inducements and the exhibition of precious stones at odd moments, attempt to obtain contracts from him and absorb a large portion of his fortune.

Tasker then entered the witness box and was examined by his second counsel, Darling. In his evidence he ran through the chronology of the transactions and stated that he was told he could have as much time as he liked to pay for the purchases. Then Sir Edward Clarke cross-examined. Tasker could not have proved a very impressive witness. On being asked about large sums of money, he replied using expressions like 'Oh, it don't matter' and 'Blowed if I know' much to the amusement of the court. Sir Edward questioned him about a diamond that he was wearing and elicited the reply that it was bought from a man known as 'Number One' under the Grand Oriental Hotel at Colombo.

Charles Lawrence, Tasker's servant, was called next and stated that his master, when he signed certain bills, was suffering from the after effects of drink. Sir Edward, in cross-examination, to the court's amusement, established that it was the previous day's drink that was the cause of the suffering. Two experts, Mr. John Jones and Mr. M. Spink, were called and they respectively valued the *Agra* at £8,000 and £10,000 and the Bow Brooch at £2,750 and £4,000.

The second day started with Mr. Findlay attempting to call a Dr. Swift to testify that the plaintiff was unfitted to make contracts but the judge ruled this inadmissible. Sir Edward then commenced the case for the defence. He stated that no more unfair way of getting out of a bargain could be devised than that adopted by the plaintiff of traducing tradesmen. The case the plaintiff had to make was one of misrepresentation but an attempt had been made to shirk this charge and to say that the plaintiff was incapable of entering into any business transactions owing to his drunken habits. To quote direct from *The Times'* law report, Sir Edward continued:

The plaintiff was surrounded by people who would have protected him if he was being attacked when in an unfit condition. Was it likely that Baron von Orsbach would have taken a man incapable through drink to Messrs. Streeter's on the occasion of the exhibition of the *Holy City* ? They would remember the plaintiff's evidence, and his handling of the pearl in Messrs. Streeter's shop, and saying that he would not express his admiration for fear of raising the price. Yet this was the young man who now was said to be incapable of entering into a bargain. They would also remember how when the plaintiff was in the witness box he said he was ill with gout, but said his head was all right. The plaintiff was not a man who, being left alone, was pursued by Mr. Rogers and induced to buy these various articles. Baron von Orsbach was present at many of the interviews, and so was the plaintiff's cousin, Mr. John Tasker, who on one occasion, filled up a cheque for £5,000 for one of the purchases. The purchase of the *Agra* diamond was not done in a single day. The bills in payment for it were brought ready drawn because the bargain had been made the day before. It was quite true that Mr. Streeter, instead of giving actual money, had given jewellery to the value of £14,000, for the *Agra* diamond, but, having done this, he (the learned counsel) submitted that Mr. Streeter was quite justified in saying that the diamond had cost him £14,000. That was no mis-representation. The plaintiff had made this bargain for the *Agra* diamond, and now he wished to get out of it. It was arranged that he should pay in bills. When Mr. Rowe and Mr. Rogers went to the hotel there was no secrecy or undue haste. The plaintiff's cousin looked at the bills before they were signed.

The report continues:

Then it was said that the plaintiff was induced to give a cheque for the *Hope* diamond, and that the defendants had done nothing in the matter. The *Hope* diamond was in the custody of the Court of Chancery. It was for sale at a price to be fixed by the Court. Mr. Rogers knew all about it. He arranged that if it could be got for £30,000, the plaintiff should have it for £32,000, Messrs. Streeter paying all the necessary legal and other expenses. Mr. Rogers applied to the Court, and began by offering £20,000, but this the Court would not accept. £25,000 would have been accepted, but before anything could be done, the plaintiff stopped his cheque, and as a consequence, the transactions all came to nothing. The defendants rightly insisted on having the cheque, as they were not going to be liable for the £25,000 and legal expenses, without full security.

In conclusion, Sir Edward submitted that the verdict of the jury should be for the defendants as to the *Agra* diamond and the Bow Brooch, also that the defendants were entitled to be paid for the pearls and the silver base for the model of the yacht which they claimed in their counterclaim.

Next Mr. Rogers was called. He stated that he had never sold anything to Tasker when he was alone. When he showed the *Agra* diamond to him, he included the receipt from Hertz and the diamond's pedigree. He added that when the *Stafford* Collection was delivered, Tasker's solicitor was present. He claimed that on the evening of the theatre party and two suppers, he showed the diamonds before supper but did not specify which ones. Under cross-examination from Mr. Findlay he denied that he was a canvasser, but a manager and buyer. He stated that in May and June 1894 he was devoting time to Tasker, selling him jewellery, as this is what he was employed to do and what Messrs. Streeter were in business to do. He received 3 per cent on sales.

Rowe was next called as a witness. He stated that he had been Streeter's secretary from 1892 until 1894. He added that he did not notice anything untoward about Tasker's behaviour and that he always behaved like a perfect gentleman. When he saw Tasker in bed, he was unwell and was not drinking but Lawrence, the servant, did bring a brandy and soda but drank it himself. He was accused by Counsel of, together with Rogers, hunting in couples.

Edwin Streeter was called on the third day. He stated that he was not involved in the actual transactions with the plaintiff. The *Agra* diamond had been in his possession for four years. It was an extraordinary stone of rose pink colour. He considered £15,000 a cheap price for it. Under cross-examination he replied that the stone's pedigree had been prepared by an Indian scholar, Colonel Birch. The pedigree spoke of the diamond being seen in the Treasury of Auranzeb in 1665. It was subsequently possessed by the Emperor Babur, the illustrious descendant of Timor of Western Tartary and founder of the Mogul Empire. Later it was worn in the head dress of Akbar and was once in possession of Nadir Shah. In further cross-examination it was pointed out that the Emperor Babur died in 1530 and that Auranzeb was born in 1618. Sir Edward, in defending this error, said pedigrees often had a hiatus. He glossed over the fact that this hiatus went back in time.

Next to be called were two experts for the defence. Mr. Arthur Dodd of 146 Leadenhall Street valued the *Agra* and the Bow Brooch at, respectively, £15,000 and £5,000. Mr. James Forster of Holborn Viaduct said he had seen the *Agra* seven years before when £20,000 was being asked for it and he put its value between £14,000 and £16,000.

The Times reported the summings up as follows:

Sir Edward Clarke Q.C., in summing up the defendants' case to the jury, asked them to say that there had been no fraud or misrepresentation on his clients' part, and that in all the defendants had done, they had acted honestly and straightforwardly. As to the entry concerning the small pink brilliant, there had been a slight mistake, but that stone was now handed over by the defendant as forming part of the *Stafford* Collection.

The *Daily Telegraph* added:

He pointed out that very few of the great diamonds of the world had a pedigree without a hiatus, but no one denied their identity. The evidence showed that the price charged for the *Agra* diamond was moderate, and it was absolutely unique in colour and size. It was traced to the possession of a man who did not die till the eighteenth century, and then disappeared absolutely for a while. After a time it reappeared in Europe, and what more reasonable account could be given of it. There was, he submitted, not a particle of evidence to support the plaintiff's allegations against the defendants.

The Times continued:

He submitted that the defendants were entitled to recover for the base of the model of the yacht and for the three pearls which they claimed in their counter-claim. As to the other transactions, they were such as should stand, and not be set aside. Mr. Darling Q.C. replied on behalf of the plaintiff, and said that Rogers and Rowe, acting on behalf of Mr. Streeter, had, so to speak, got possession of the plaintiff and induced him to buy jewellery when he was in such a condition as to be no match for them. They had well watched their opportunity. The learned counsel then dealt with the Bow Brooch, and said that the plaintiff had never purchased it at all. If the defendants' story with regard to the *Hope* diamond transaction were true - viz., that it could have been purchased for £25,000 - then they would have made an enormous profit of £7,000 on that on which they had not spent a penny of their own money. The learned counsel submitted this was only one instance of the sort of contracts into which this foolish young man had been drawn. He asked the jury to say that £300 was enough for the model of the yacht, including the base. £300 was also owing for some pearls, and this the plaintiff would pay, making £600 in all. One of the bills for £1,000 given by the plaintiff had been negotiated, and that would pay for the yacht and the pearls and leave £400 to be returned to the plaintiff. Dealing with the transaction as to the seven brilliants which took place after supper at the plaintiff's hotel, the learned counsel observed that it was strange for honest jewellers to carry about costly diamonds and produce them from their pockets for sale at such a time. He further asked the jury to say that the dealings with regard to the small pink brilliant, which at one time was said to be included in the *Stafford* Collection, and at another, in the seven brilliants transaction, were suspicious in the extreme. As to the *Agra* diamond, the defendant would have the jury believe that its value was not increased by its having a pedigree. Why then did the defendant go to the trouble of employing Colonel Birch and getting a pedigree drawn up at all ? The plaintiff had bought the *Agra* diamond, relying on its pedigree. In his (the learned counsel's) view, never had there been a more ridiculous pedigree of a diamond than the one provided by the defendants. The defendants had said that they had given £14,000 for the *Agra* diamond, but when the transaction by which it had come into Mr. Streeter's possession was examined, it was found that it was impossible to fix upon the true value given by him, as the diamond had been purchased by an exchange of goods, and not by money, and thus no real estimate could be properly fixed. In conclusion, he asked the jury to say that the transaction into which the plaintiff had been induced to enter should be set aside, and that the bills and the cheques for £51,625 should be returned.

The learned judge summed up on the fourth day. He stated that the case revolved around alleged fraud. The incapacity through drink of the plaintiff was a side issue. There was no evidence of fraud against Mr. Streeter himself, as he had nothing to do with the actual sales, but he was liable for acts done by his agents. In conclusion his Lordship said that morally there was much to be deprecated in the way Mr. Rogers had acted; but they were not there to rebuke a want of morals, but to decide questions on strict legal principles. The question was whether the representation made to the plaintiff that the goods were of the value put on them was false and fraudulent.

The jury adjourned at 11.30 a.m. While they were out, Mr. Findlay took the opportunity of raising a point with the judge. He said that such was the interest in the case that other members of the Bar had sought to enter the court but had been, on the directions of the judge, sent upstairs to the public gallery. The judge replied that the courtroom was becoming dangerously overcrowded and those not professionally involved must go upstairs. The jury returned at 3.30 p.m. and found for Tasker in regard to the *Agra* diamond and the stand for the silver yacht. They found for Streeter in regard to the Egg Shaped Pearl, Brazilian Stone Diamond Ring, Model of the Holy City, Stafford Collection, Black and White Pearls and the Bow Brooch. The contracts for the *Hope* diamond and seven brilliants were to be set aside. There was considerable confusion when the verdict was delivered and Mr. Justice Lord Pollock announced that in view of the difficulty in adjusting the figures he would

DESCRIPTION	PRICE £	SUBJECT OF		JURY FINDINGS FOR	
		Claim by Tasker	Counter Claim Streeter	Tasker	Streeter
Egg Shaped Pearl	500				•
Brazilian Stone Diamond Hoop	300				•
Model of the Gates of the Holy City	1,500				•
Model of the *Zingara* Stand	300 150			Not Disputed •	
Hope Diamond	32,000				Contract Nul
Stafford Collection	10,000				•
Agra Diamond	15,000	•		•	
Diamond Earring & Brooch	6,500				•
3 Pearls (1 Pink, 1 Black, 1 White)	300		•		•
Diamond Bow Brooch	5,000	•			•
7 Large Brilliants	15,000			Contract Nul	
Miscellaneous	450				
Sub Total	**£ 87,000**				
Other Undisputed Transactions	£ 13,500				
TOTAL	**£100,500**				

SUMMARY OF THE PIECES INVOLVED IN THE TASKER CASE

announce how the judgment would be entered next day. On the next day, an agreed statement was read out, which balanced out the various transactions according to the jury's verdict.

One does not know the secrets of the jury room but it may be that the jury's verdict reflected their thoughts on a fair compromise between the parties, bearing in mind their conduct and behaviour, rather than a strict legal deduction from all the facts. It has not been possible to trace Mr. Tasker after these events, so it is not known if he pursued into oblivion his career of a rake or if he embarked on another. The *Daily Telegraph* published a long sarcastic article on the case, congratulating Mr. Tasker on discovering a new way of getting rid of the incumbrance of a fortune in the shortest possible space of time and at the smallest possible expenditure of effort ! The paper went on to say that gambling on the Turf, speculating on the Stock Exchange and producing plays at West End theatres had already been tried but purchasing pedigree diamonds was totally novel. They added, however, that to rival Mr. Tasker one should make purchases through a general haze of alcoholic exhilaration. Other papers observed that Tasker might have used his fortune for the benefit of the poor. His solicitors rushed to his defence. In a letter published in the *Globe*, they stated that such critics had no knowledge of their client. They continued: 'His generosity to the poor was unstinted and upon the score of benevolence he is a pattern to many who would venture to criticise him.'

The same day Oscar Wilde issued a writ on the Marquis of Queensbury so the Tasker case faded into the recesses of the public's memory and another caught alight to capture their interest.

CHAPTER EIGHT

EMERALDS FROM EGYPT

In 1892 a new front was put into the shop which the *Watchmaker, Jeweller and Silversmith* described as handsome, substantial and an immense improvement on the old one.[1] May 1895 saw the registration of a limited company, Streeter and Co. Ltd., to be the new vehicle of the business. Edwin was to have 45,300 of the new shares, his wife 1,000, 500 were to go to each of his children, Florence, Violet, Beatrice, Louise, Cecil and Saville and 100 each to two outsiders, William Townsend and Robert Brockman. Two children, George who was out in Broome, Western Australia managing the pearling station, and Ethel, were omitted from this distribution. It may be that they were out of favour at the time. In December of that year, 20,000 extra shares were issued to the public and they were all taken up. The Directors of the Company were Edwin Streeter (Chairman), Lieut. Col. Arthur Collins, G. E. J. Manners, Capt. F.G.J. Manners and Secretary and Sub-Manager, C.F. Streeter.[2] Not surprisingly, considering the Montana ruby affair, the interest of the press was aroused. The *Saturday Review* on 14 December 1895 commented, 'We view with grave distrust Mr. Edwin W. Streeter's efforts to finance his Bond Street business by turning it into a Limited Company.' Their main objections were that profits were given as an average of £7,000 for the last seven years with no breakdown for each year and with no accountant's report. Also they observed that there was no need to sell the business as the proprietor was not retiring. But on this occasion it was Streeter who was on sure ground and the Press whose arguments were shaky.

Smiles & Co., solicitors to the issue, replied to the criticisms.[3] The accountants, George Dixey and Co., they said, had put their name to the prospectus and this was as good as a certificate. In fact, the mechanics of the operation were similar to many new issues today. The proprietor of the business, which he had built up over many years, was selling part of it to the

---

1 *W.J.S.* 1 December 1892.

2 Cecil Streeter always worked as a 'backroom boy'. He was Secretary of Streeter & Co. Ltd. and his only rise to prominence was when, in 1901, he wrote to *The Times* in defence of the District Messenger Company. Streeter used this reliable firm to carry jewellery all over London but its existence was threatened by the Post Office, enforcing its monopoly.

3 *Saturday Review.* 4 January 1896.

public so that he could realise some capital. The soundness of the issue was to be proved by the actual profits of the next six years, which were: £8,850; £9,200; £9,200; £6,400; £4,300; and £7,100. An average of £7,508 per year.[1]

In the closing years of the century, Edwin was to see his children start off in married life. The first was Louise, who in 1897, married Julius d'Adhémar de Labaume, the 35-year-old son of a French aristocrat, Count Jules-Esprit d'Adhémar de Labaume.[2]   Julius gave his occupation on the marriage certificate as Timber Surveyor. The next year Cecil married Winifred Lock, the daughter of George Lock, whose occupation was variously given as 'Art Decorator' and 'Art Expert.' Beatrice was to marry Winifred's brother, Harold Lock, an electrical engineer, in 1901. George returned from Australia in 1898 and married Blanche Gold, daughter of Sir Charles Gold, one of the first partners in W. & A. Gilbey, the wine and spirit merchants.

The firm had a diamond cutting workshop at 16 Glasshouse Street under the management of Leopold Claremont. Leopold was the youngest son of a doctor. Most of his elder brothers went into medicine but on the advice of Edwin, who may have been a family friend, he was apprenticed to R.C. Nickold of 12 Frith Street, Soho, who was then regarded as the foremost exponent of the trade. On the expiry of the articles, Claremont was offered the position of head of the firm's gem cutting department and, as we saw earlier, did demonstrations in the shop window. In 1895, Claremont took over the department and in 1899, with an American partner, James Ward, moved to 38 Conduit Street, next to Streeter's old premises. He was to publish a book, *The Gem Cutter's Craft*, in 1906.[3]

---

1 *Stock Exchange Year Books.* 1897-1903.

2 The d'Adhémar family is an interesting one. The de Labaume branch hails from Montpellier. Jules-Esprit came to London as a diplomat and, after political changes at home, decided to stay. The French branch married into the Polignac family, ancestors of the Princes of Monaco. The last male representative of the branch in France was Count Charles who was an Officer in the French Navy and then became a painter. During the war he imprudently allied himself with the Vichy Government and he and his wife were killed during the 1945 Liberation.

A slight estrangement arose between Louise and her family after her marriage because her husband was a Roman Catholic. Matters were made worse because one of her brothers mismanaged the investments in her marriage settlement and Edwin had to make up the loss to the extent of £1,950 in his will.

The male line of this branch has died out in France but thrives in such divers places as East Anglia, Washington D.C., U.S.A. and Perth, Western Australia.

3 Culme, *Directory of Silversmiths*, pp.84-85. Norman Hurst, *Women at Home*.

LEOPOLD A. CLAREMONT.
Fig. 99.

One might have thought that, at the age of 63, Edwin would have learned his lesson about quixotically backing mining companies. It was not to be. In 1897, the year of the liquidation of the Sapphire and Ruby Mine Company of Montana, he despatched H.W. Seton-Karr[1] to Egypt to explore the ancient emerald workings of Sikait and Zabbara. This gentleman brought home a quantity of rough emerald, some of which yielded stones of excellent quality. Edwin considered it unlikely that the mines, which were so extensively worked by the ancients, were exhausted so he applied to the Egyptian Government for a concession.[2] The concession was granted and in July 1899 a contract was negotiated with a mining engineer called Kelly for the hire of his yacht *Ariade* and six crew. The expedition never left and in the following year Kelly sued in the High Court to recover his expenses. Edward Carson appeared for Kelly and Rufus Isaacs for Streeter. Mr. Justice Mathew found that Streeter's defence, that the contract was void on the grounds of common mistakes by both parties, could not be sustained and he was ordered to pay £600 damages.[3]

In spite of this inauspicious start, the Egyptian Gold and Gem Syndicate was formed in 1903 with Edwin as Chairman and his son Cecil one of the directors.[4] Edwin took up 5,833 of the 36,230 £1 shares issued. Two years later he had to advance the company £4,000. But it did not prosper. He resigned a year later and in 1907, on the grounds that 'the company cannot continue by reason of its liabilities', it was voluntarily wound up.[5]

In 1905 Edwin was seventy-one and the failure of the Egyptian Syndicate may have finally persuaded him to retire. Also his eyesight was failing. On one recent occasion he had bought a pair of pearl drops for £1,000 and discovered later that one had a crack and that they were worth only £100.[6] In a letter to Lord Rothschild dated 29 January 1903 he stated, 'during the last two years my eyesight has been very precarious and I have had to undergo several operations.'

---

1 Haywood Seton-Karr, b.1859. Lt. Gordon Highlanders. Discovered prehistoric flint mines in Somalia.

2 *Precious Stones and Gems.* 6th edition, p.207.

3 *The Times.* 26 April 1900.

4 The other directors were A.C. Bicknell and G.O. Haig.

5 *Stock Exchange Year Book* and P.R.O. R1890/10191.

6 Obituary, *Hampstead & Highgate Express.* 20 October 1923.

None of his sons were willing or able to carry on the business. Harry had died on a pearling expedition in 1886. George, then aged 42, had spent much of his working life in the tropics, was now of independent means, and had recently retired with his growing family to a small estate at Thorley, Hertfordshire. Saville, aged 27, had qualified as a solicitor but nothing is known of his subsequent career. Cecil, aged 33, was the only one currently working in the firm but a year later we find him with William Payne & Co., Jewellers of 163 New Bond Street.[1] It is possible that the Egyptian Gem Syndicate had drained son as well as father of capital and that he was in no position to take up the business.

Streeter & Co. Ltd. was put into voluntary liquidation in March 1905, the preference shares receiving twenty shillings in the pound but the founders' and ordinary shares, only twelve shillings and sixpence in the pound. The goodwill, premises and some of the stock were purchased by Lacloche Frères Ltd., a firm founded in Paris in 1897 and having branches in San Sebastian, Biarritz and Madrid.[2] They moved to 2 New Bond Street. Some of the business moved with Cecil to William Payne & Co. In the 1905 *Kelly's Directory* they are listed as just watchmakers but in the 1908 edition, Streeter & Co. Ltd. are marked as transferred to William Payne & Co., 163 New Bond Street and that firm are now described as watchmakers and jewellers. In 1909 Kirkby and Bunn of 17 Cork Street took over William Payne & Co. and until at least 1926, they advertised that they were the successors to Streeter & Co. Ltd. Also Debenham and Freebody took over a quantity of the smaller priced articles of stock.[3]

The only interest Edwin maintained was in 12 Clifford Street, the side entrance to the premises, which was let to Miss Slater Ltd., Costumiers. Finnigans, makers of trunks and dressing bags, took over 18 New Bond Street. Today the site has been redeveloped and is the headquarters of Air India.

An indication of the size of the business is given by the fact that, as well as three firms taking over the stock, there was a sale at Christie's on 22 February 1905. The highlight of the sale was the *Agra* diamond, which has been dealt with in an earlier chapter.[4] Also sold were: a pearl necklace composed of 50 graduated pearls of fine orient with single brilliant snap - £1,200 to Eyles; a pearl and brilliant cluster pendant or brooch with fine pear-shaped drop - £520

---

1 *Post Office Directory* 1906.

2 Culme, *Directory of Silversmiths.*

3 *The Times.* 6 February 1895.

4 See also Appendix 3.

to Banbury; pearl necklace of 55 graduated pearls and single brilliant snap - £1,200 to Slazenger; and another, composed of a row of small pearls and nine large pearls - £1,950 to Pearce. The total of the 127 lots amounted to £19,491.

On retirement Streeter firstly moved to 15 Buckingham Palace Gardens and then to 49 Compayne Gardens, Hampstead, a modest Victorian semi-detached house, which still stands, and where he was to remain for the rest of his life. A memoir of him around this time is provided by Mrs. Patience Chester-Master, eldest daughter of George. She wrote in 1986:

I can remember very little about my Streeter grandparents and saw them very seldom. My Father never really talked much about them, although the Streeter aunts often stayed at Thorley, but his two brothers never. Vaguely we were made to believe they were not much good.

The first time I remember going to see my grandparents, I am nearly sure they were living in Regent's Park, but after then it was always Hampstead. The address, I believe, was 49 Compayne Gardens.

When we were children, one of the great excitements of Christmas was opening a huge portmanteau of presents from London. It was always opened in my Father's library on Christmas Eve, and as far as I can remember, they were always expensive presents. I have still got a children's tea set that I was given.

The house in Hampstead was dark and full of heavy Victorian furniture, and I hated it. Grandpa seldom appeared (I think he suffered from asthma). When I went there, I spent the time with the Aunts in their rooms; Flo, Violet and Ethel.

There was one excitement, a kind of box doll's house full of shining bright things when a light was turned on, and we were always shown this as a great treat.

My Father told me that his Father could never say 'No' to anybody who wanted to borrow money if it was anything to do with mining, and therefore was always giving money to people who thought they were going to make a fortune, which never came off. That is the way I understood he lost all his wealth. Certainly when they both died, the Aunts were left with practically nothing.

Fig. 100. The Gates of the Holy City
Presented to the Goldsmiths' Company in 1910

My Father never talked about the shop in Bond Street or about jewellery, and I do not think my Mother had any very special jewellery, although the shop was still there in 1898 when they were married.

I have no recollection of the sale of the house in Hampstead, and do not know the date. I cannot remember anything coming to Thorley if all the contents were sold, but I might have been away at school.

Edwin lived on in reduced circumstances with his wife and three unmarried daughters. However, he had funds enough in 1910 to commission and present to the Goldsmiths' Company, together with four books from his library, another model of the *Gates of the Holy City* - this one by Alfred Godfrey, in silver-gilt with precious stones as described in the Book of Revelation.[1] In 1918 his wife died and in 1919, he presented the remains of his collection of books to the Goldsmiths' Company. He had had an offer for them from Jeffrey's of New York but wished them to remain in England.[2]

The author has in his possession a case containing three jeweller's tools. They consist of a shovel and a shovel-cum-tweezers, both with the inscription 'Streeter Lombard St. 1674 and 18 Bond St. 1874.' The first part of the inscription being in an older style script. Also there is a miniature ladle, pick and tweezers all attached to a ring. Stuck into the case is the following writing in E.W. Streeter's hand:

This shovel and pair of diamond tongs belonged to Mr. Streeter of Lombards who was apprenticed to Mydleton, the goldsmith, of the City of London. He was related to the artist, Streeter, who was knighted by Henry VIII on the field of the Cloth of Gold - see Lodge's *Landed Gentry*. These tools were used by Mr. Streeter, the author of *Precious Stones and Gems*, *Pearls and Pearling Life* etc. He wishes them to be retained in the family of Mr. Streeter.

With this small book[3] - they may be handed over to the first Streeter of the family who becomes a Diamond and Pearl merchant or a prominent goldsmith.

---

[1] This could not have been the same model of the Holy Gates as the one involved in the Tasker case. The earlier model was sold to Tasker as part of the settlement and the later one is clearly date stamped.

[2] Correspondence in possession of the Goldsmiths' Company.

[3] This book has been lost.

British Museum

Fig. 101. E. W. Streeter's Tool Case showing notes.

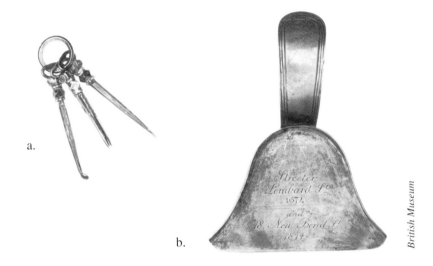

British Museum

Back View

Front View

Fig. 102. E.W.Streeter's Jeweller's Tools
a. pick and tweezers
b. shovel
c. and d. shovel-cum-tweezers

I wish him to join the Guild of Goldsmiths to whom I presented part of my Library on these subjects.

With these tools I leave the copyright of all my books viz. P.S & Gems, Pearls & P. Life. Gt diamonds of the World, The Legal Regulation of Gold and other works. Edwin W. Streeter.

The opinion of the British Museum is that the tools are Victorian, so the inscription 'Streeter Lombard St. 1674' must be false. As to the writing, there was a Walter Streeter apprenticed first to Thomas Harris in 1671 and then to William Middleton. He received his freedom in 1680 but there is no evidence that he was an ancestor of Edwin. There was no artist Streeter knighted on the Field of Cloth of Gold. The reference must be from a cutting in an old book in the family about one Guillim Streeter, who painted an anamorphic[1] portrait of Edward VI acquired by the National Portrait Gallery in 1902. However, this artist was in fact a Fleming, William Scrots, also known as Gullim Stretes.[2] There is no such book as Lodge's *Landed Gentry*. This collection of tools must have been annotated after the first lot of books were donated to the Goldsmiths' Company and all together they illustrate a mind straying into the realms of fantasy.

A letter from Edwin's solicitors written in 1922 gives some indication of the reduced circumstances in which he was living. It shows that he had outstanding loans to insurance companies and that his annual income was £1,084. £804 of this was provided by an annuity from his son, George. He died peacefully in his ninetieth year on 11 October 1923, leaving in his will £8,493 gross, £3,379 net. His ashes were taken to the Church of St. Margaret the Queen, Buxted, where he had had his country seat, and interred in the churchyard. His name was added to those of his wife and son on the brass memorial plaque on the wall of the south aisle, which reads:

In loving memory of Harry Edwin Streeter eldest son of Edwin William and Sarah Streeter who died 24 February 1886 his 26th birthday whilst in charge of his father's pearling fleet. His body rests in Fremantle Church Yard, Western Australia. Also in memory of the Parents of the Above who departed this life.

---

1 Anamorphic pictures are distorted when viewed from the front and only appear normal when viewed from a certain angle.

2 I am grateful to Andrea Gall of the National Portrait Gallery for this information.

Sarah Grainger Streeter
Nov 21 1918

Edwin William Streeter F.R.G.S. M.R.A.S.
Oct 11 1923

whose ashes are interred in this churchyard.

Edwin Streeter lived a long, colourful, eventful life. He achieved and lost fame and wealth but neither of these were objectives. His financial failures were due to his not being interested in money but in the idea of expeditions and enterprises, the exciting prospects of which at times impaired his judgement. The foremost motivation in his life was his passion for and interest in precious stones, pearls and gold.

LETTER REPORTING CONDITIONS IN SOUTH AFRICA
FROM
THOMAS TOBIN

Diamond Fields,
Pniel,
Vaal River,
South Africa.

13 April 1871

To E .W. Streeter Esq.

Dear Sir,

You will be glad to hear that we have arrived safely at the termination of our outward journey; and no doubt it will be interesting to yourself as well as the general public to have a record of our first impressions and a brief description of the diamond fields of South Africa.

Let me preface my remarks by stating; all that has been represented in the English papers regarding the richness of the country on the banks of the Vaal River in diamond wealth is fully borne out in reality. The picture drawn has not been too highly coloured but, at the best, diamond seeking is a lottery and it cannot be too strongly impressed on the minds of all who are purporting to make the fields a scene of their future labours, that wealth is essential to beget wealth, and unless prepared to lose in the hope of winning, they had better refrain from the venture. From my short experience, anyone wishing to visit the fields in the hope of diamond finding, must come prepared with an income for at least six months. Success in some degree he is then almost certain of achieving.

We reached the fields on 20 March 1871, having left England on 23 November 1870. But a large portion of the interval was spent in exploring the Vaal district and its geological formation. Nevertheless, the journey is invariably a tedious one and if inconvenience and annoyance bear any weight, the intending digger will soon find a termination to his project long before reaching the fields. Contrasted with a long and dreary period spent in passing through a heated, sandy and barren desert, the first sight of the Vaal River presents a lively and cheering view to the traveller. It is not until within a few miles that the river itself is visible, by reason of high banks which encompass it for a long distance in either direction, but the noise of busy cradles rocking the diamondiferous soil for a thousand diggers, the rush of the rapid stream and the occasional encountering of a veritable digger in full costume, soon assure the traveller that he is nearing the diamond fields; in a few short hours he is walking over countless perhaps priceless gems.

The Vaal River, as its name implies, is turbid and by reason of the rapid current contains, at all times of the year, a large amount of muddy matter. The banks, as already described, are elevated on each side and generally studded over their surfaces with large boulders, rendering locomotion difficult and in some parts, impassable. Evidently the river has in ages past been much larger than at present. Indeed, the vast tract of country drained by it and the rapid falls (this locality being some 4,000 feet above sea level), causes it in the summer to be a grand stream of water some 400 or 500 yards in width. While in the dry winter season it dwindles into a mere brook, in many places fordable on horse or foot.

There can be but one opinion as to the geological formation of the district: at every turn evidence is afforded of igneous action, the surface of the ground shows undoubted traces of volcanic disturbances, added to which the stones, the pebbles and debris on the river banks and elsewhere, all conduce to the fact of their origin being by fire or metamorphic action. The manner in which this action has affected the surface of the ground is through, what to geologists is known as 'trap'. The sedimentary deposits of the districts having been disturbed, broken up and greenstone in a molten form exuded which, flowing over the surface, has burned or calcined the underlying strata into metamorphic rocks. Everywhere is this greenstone visible.

Sometimes a dyke occurs across a river bed, elevating portions several feet and causing very picturesque water falls. At others, it appears as immense water-worn boulders lying on the bank and in the bed of the rivers. Now Pniel, which had been the most productive camp in the whole of the field, bears distinct traces of having been at one time the actual bed of the river but through volcanic disturbance, thrown up to its present elevated position, causing the river to find for itself a course around its foot. Hence it is only reasonable, from this and other equally conclusive evidence, to surmise that there are more gems in the river bed than on its banks.

The means employed by the diggers are of the most primitive nature; system is ignored and to a stranger it appears marvellous that any 'finds' could possibly emanate from such rude contrivances as those used on the river bank. The process generally employed consists of first digging out the ground, second by carting it down by bullock waggon to the river bank and thirdly washing and sorting soil, separating the diamonds from the wash. There is little or no difficulty in obtaining a licence to dig. A space about two feet square is allotted as a 'claim' on the payment of a sum varying from 5/- to 30/- per month. Sometimes the claim turns out fortunate and after having found several stones, he sells it for a large sum. Generally a claim will yield something. But the hard work and anxiety often wears out the patience of the owner and he abandons it for another more promising. Thus it is that hundreds of claims are duly left unworked and new camps established up and down the river. Can the South African diamond ever be said to be exhausted under such undisciplined procedure? Independently of this, a claim is seldom dug deeper than about 18 inches or two feet. Exception at Pniel and there diamonds are found on the bedrock some 20 to 30 feet below the surface. There is every reason to suppose that the same results will apply to other parts when engineering skill is brought to bear in the operations.

The extent of the fields at the present time is about 30 miles of the river line east and west. The lower camp - Dutoits Pan - is about 25 miles south. The principal camps are on the river banks and of their number, Pniel is the seat of government and commerce; opposite Pniel is Klep Drift where, to avoid being undermined by the diggings, the colonial merchants are erecting their stores. The area of the fields is daily being augmented and there seems to be limit neither to quantity nor quality in the yield of diamonds. A weekly publication exists called the *Diamond News* but the idiosyncrasies of the diggers prevent anything like a truthful record of the prosperity and progress of the enterprise. Another fact is worthy of note. For the most part the diggers are respectable, well-to-do men and their best 'finds' are kept by them, while the inferior stones are sold to defray current expenses. Hence the markets have, at present, had but little opportunity of testing the comparative value of the South African diamonds.

A few words as to the social bearing of the fields. As a whole, a better conducted community many an European Government cannot boast. Order and discipline prevails to an extent almost incredible. Both English and Dutch law is dealt but as a rule, the majority of the diggers prefer the former. No doubt by this time you have heard of the dispute pending the right of absolute rule on the fields. For many years previous to the discovery of the diamond wealth, the whole tract of diamond land had no owner. Now it had several aspirants to possess it. Meantime the English and Dutch rival each other in meting out justice and vigilance. Watching the interests of their respective subjects. Some day, let us hope that the

English will assume authority over a country at one time abandoned as an encumbrance but now promising to become one of the brightest pearls in the British crown.

In conclusion, and as illustrating practically the bearing of this report after three weeks experience of the diamond fields, our party have found two diamonds of pure water and good shape, both of which I intend forwarding by an early mail to England - meantime anticipating every success to our expedition.

I am, Dear Sir,
Yours very sincerely,

Thos. Wm. Tobin
Sec. Royal Poly Intn.

P.S. I open this a second time to say that we have unearthed a diamond - 4 carats in weight. Yours of March 9th has just arrived to hand.

At the end of the letter the following is added, probably by E. W. Streeter after the letter had arrived in London.

The accompanying note may serve to show how quickly a rich prize may fall to the lot of the diamond seeker. Mr. Tobin's foreman of works, Mr. Hilliard, was a short time since addressed by a digger who had been but a few days at work on a claim which he had established adjoining Mr. Tobin's and requested to give his opinion as to the quality of a stone just discovered. The new find was at once pronounced to be a diamond, which on being weighed, proved to be 96 carats, worth approximately £100,000 according to Jeffery's scale.

HALLMARKS & TRADEMARKS

Edwin William STREETER.
Gold worker.
22nd November 1882.

Edwin William STREETER.
Gold worker.
24th February 1898.

Edwin William STREETER.
Gold worker.
22nd November 1882.

Edwin William STREETER
Gold worker.
3rd April 1873.

Edwin William STREETER.
Gold worker.
19th March 1878.

STREETER & CO. LTD.
Gold & Silver workers.
27th July 1899.
entered by Edwin W. Streeter,
Managing Director.

STREETER & CO. LTD.
Gold & Silver workers.
17th October 1899.

Fig. 103. The Hallmarks used by E.W. Streeter
as registered with the Goldsmiths' Company.

Also on page 5 of the 60th edition of the catalogue, various marks are described thus:

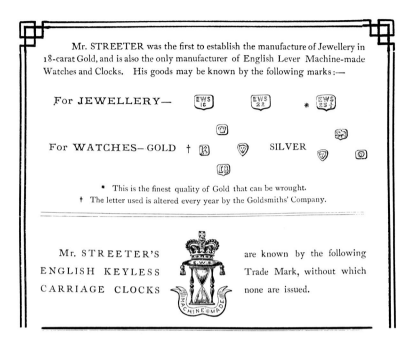

Fig. 104.

In some pieces, the hourglass mark is found in a simpler form showing just the actual glass.

HISTORY OF THE AGRA DIAMOND

Christie's

Fig. 105. The Agra Diamond.

The best account of the *Agra* diamond's history is found in Ian Balfour's *Famous Diamonds* (2nd edition). Humanyu, son of the first Mogul Emperor, Babur, took Agra in 1526. Balfour speculates that the stone was with those given to Humanyu as a token of thanks by the family of the slain Rajah of Gwalior for the sparing of their lives. Col. Birch's pedigree states that the stone was owned by Babur and taken by him from an Indian Rajah at the battle of Agra. Later it was to be found in the head dress of his grandson Akbar, the third Emperor. Also it was lodged in the treasury of Auranzeb, Akbar's great grandson and the seventh Emperor. It was pointed out in the cross-examination in the Tasker case, that the Birch pedigree has inconsistent dates, in that he has the stone passing from Auranzeb, who was born in 1618, to Babur, who died in 1530. The pedigree claims that the stone was in the possession of Nadir Shah. Nadir Shah, son of a maker of sheepskin coats, became successively a robber chief and King of Persia. He sacked Delhi in 1739, seized the Imperial treasures, but did not occupy the capital and contented himself with annexing some western provinces. A number of the treasures were recaptured when Nadir got into difficulty while crossing a river on the way home. The *Agra* could have been amongst these.

We next pick up the story when the Duke of Brunswick bought the stone for 348,000 francs (*c.* £14,000) in 1844 from George Blogg of the London firm of diamond merchants Blogg and Martin. These details come from the Brunswick collection catalogue which mentions that the stone was taken by Babur in Agra in 1526. The catalogue does not say how the stone came from India to

England. One account is printed in *The Times* on 6 February 1905 as a preview to the Streeter sale of 22 February. We quote directly from the newspaper.

One article alone will stamp the forthcoming sale as one of unique interest - namely, the famous *Agra* diamond. This diamond derives its name from the fact that it was taken to the Battle of Agra in 1526 by the Emperor Babur, who was the founder of the Mongul Empire in India. The modern history of the diamond was told to Mr. Streeter in the summer of 1906 by the Marquis of Donegall, and it is as follows:-

The Marquis remarked that he was in Agra in 1857 when the diamond was taken from the King of Delhi, being at the time engaged as secretary and belonging to the same regiment as the young officer who obtained possession of the diamond. It was resolved amongst them to smuggle it home to England rather than give it up and share in the loot money. The question arose how were they to get it home? No one seemed to be able to hit upon a method that would be likely to meet with success until the last evening previous to the departure of the regiment. During the course of dinner, the youngest subaltern suddenly jumped up and said, 'I have it; we will conceal the diamond in a horse ball and make the horse swallow it.' This met with general approbation, a ball was secured, the inside scooped out, the diamond inserted, and the end stopped up and the horse made to swallow it. When the regiment reached the port of embarcation, the horse was taken ill and had to be shot. The diamond was taken from his stomach and brought over to England. It was subsequently sold to the Duke of Brunswick and since then, it has been reduced from a 46 carat stone to a 31½ carats in order to get rid of the black spots in it, and it is now the most perfect and brilliant diamond of a lovely rose pink colour.

The Marquis dates this story in 1857, when he was aged 25, plain George Augustus Hamilton and serving with the 6th Foot. The Brunswick catalogue states that the stone was purchased in 1844. There are four explanations. Either the Marquis or the Duke has got his dates wrong, there are two different stones, or the horse ball story is a myth. The reader is left to make up his own mind but he may be helped in this exercise by *The Times*, who backtracked on their story as can be seen by this paragraph published on 20 February 1905.

The Streeter Jewels. This very fine collection of jewels will be on view at Messrs. Christie's today, the sale taking place on Wednesday. There are in all 127 lots, the famous *Agra* diamond, to which reference was made in

The Times recently, being the concluding lot of the sale. With regard to the history of this diamond, some of the published details appear to require modifying, but the quality of the stone is of the highest.

The Duke's collection was sold in 1874 by Rossel & Fils in Geneva and he died in 1884. In the Tasker case, the expert James Forster states that he saw the *Agra* in 1888 when £20,000 was being asked for it.

By 1891 the stone was in the possession of Messrs. Hertz & Co. of Paris, from whom Streeter acquired it, exchanging pearls worth £15,000 for the *Agra* and £1,000 cash. After the abortive sale to Tasker, the stone remained in Streeter's museum until the sale of 1905. A large crowd was attracted, including a number of Indian gentlemen. The first bid for the *Agra* was £1,000 and at £5,100, it was knocked down to Max Meyer of Hatton Garden, with S. H. Harris the underbidder. The price of £5,100 compares unfavourably to the £15,000 asked of Tasker for the stone.

The *Agra* next appeared, together with the *Hope*, at the Paris sale of Saloman Habib's in June 1909 and was subsequently to be found in the collection of Louis Winans, the son of an American railway magnate who built the line from St. Petersburg to Moscow. A descendant of Winans, who inherited the diamond in 1927, placed it for sale with Christie's in June 1990. During the war his collection had been kept for safety in an iron casket in the garden. It was sold to the Ciba Corporation of Hong Kong for a hammer price of £3,600,000.

BIBLIOGRAPHY

Bain, Mary Albertus. *Full Fathom Five*. Perth, 1982.

Balfour, Ian. *Famous Diamonds*. London, 1987. 2nd edn., 1992.

Bury, Shirley. *Jewellery 1789-1910: The International Era*. London, 1991.

Bartlett, Norman. *The Pearl Seekers*. London, 1954.

Clockmakers' Company. *Catalogue of the Museum of the Clockmakers' Company*. London, 1902.

Crosthwaite, C.E. *The Pacification of Burma*. London, 1912. reprinted 1968.

Culme, John. *Directory of Gold & Silversmiths* (2 vols.). London, 1987.

Edwards, Hugh. *Port of Pearls: A History of Broome*. Perth, 1983.

Farn, Alexander. *Pearls*. London, 1986.

Gill, J.O. *Gill's Index to Journals, Articles and Books relating to Gems and Jewellery*. Santa Monica, 1978.

Lockwood, Douglas. *The Front Door: Darwin 1869-1969*. Adelaide, 1968.

Roberts, Brian. *The Diamond Magnates*. London, 1972.

Stewart, A.T.Q. *The Pagoda War*. London, 1972.

Streeter, E.W. *Precious Stones and Gems*. London, 1877.
- *Great Diamonds of the World*. London, 1882.
- *Pearls and Pearling Life*. London, 1886.

Tait, Hugh (ed.). *The Art of the Jeweller: A Catalogue of the Hull Grundy Gift to the British Museum* (2 vols.). London, 1984.

Tarling, Nicholas. *Sulu and Sabah*. Kuala Lumpur, 1978.

Wheatcroft, Geoffrey. *The Randlords*. London, 1985.

PICTURE CREDITS

Picture credits have been mentioned alongside the illustrations. Particular thanks are due to Capt. Anthony Perriam, 1st Battalion, the Black Watch, for arranging the photography of the Presentation Piece owned by his Regiment. Also Ted Donohoe of Donohoe, Davies Mews, W.1, Wartski, D.S. Lavender, Asprey and Nicholas and Olivia Gerrish have been most helpful.

Edwin Streeter's 1885 Jewellery Catalogue has been reprinted by The Matching Press and is available from 1 Waterman's End, Matching, Harlow, Essex CM17 0RQ at a price of £15 including postage and packing.

INDEX

Page numbers in bold type refer to illustrations